This book is presented to:

_____

This family devotional is
dedicated to my mum, Betty Walsh.
My love for the Word of God
began at your feet.

Copyright © 2015 by Sheila Walsh
Published by B&H Publishing Group, Nashville, Tennessee

By Sheila Walsh with Jean Fischer

ISBN: 978-1-4336-8804-1

Dewey Decimal Classification: C242

Subject Heading: BIBLE / DEVOTIONAL LITERATURE / FAMILY

Unless otherwise marked, all Scripture references are taken from the
Holman Christian Standard Bible (HCSB). Copyright © 1999, 2000, 2002, 2003,
2009 by Holman Bible Publishers, Nashville Tennessee. All rights reserved.

Scriptures marked KJV are taken from the *King James Version*. Scriptures marked NIV
are taken from *Holy Bible, New International Version*®, NIV® Copyright ©1973,
1978, 1984, 2011 by Biblica, Inc.®. Used by permission. All rights reserved worldwide.
Scriptures marked NLT are taken from the *New Living Translation*, copyright© 1996,
2004, 2007, 2013 by Tyndale House Foundation. Used by permission of Tyndale
House Publishers Inc., Carol Stream, Illinois 60188. All rights reserved.

All rights reserved. Printed in Heshan, Guangdong, China, February 2017.

2 3 4 5 6 7 8   21 20 19 18 17

THE BIBLE IS MY BEST FRIEND

FAMILY DEVOTIONAL

52 DEVOTIONS FOR FAMILIES

SHEILA WALSH

WITH JEAN FISCHER · ILLUSTRATED BY SARAH HORNE

B&H KID

Nashville, Tennessee

LETTER TO FAMILIES

Homework, housework, soccer practice, birthday parties—with today's schedules, I know it's tough for families to find time in God's Word *and* time with each other. But studying the Bible together can be the best quality time there is, especially with this unique devotional.

Each week you'll find a devotion to connect families to the Bible and to each other at the same time. Keep reading, and you'll find one main message: Whether you're a parent or a kid, the Bible is your best friend. It's your way to learn about God's love for you and His plan to save you through His Son, Jesus. It can be your guide and your comfort, no matter where you go.

Use these pages to explore God's Word together through memory verses, Scripture scavenger hunts, weekly challenges, and a good dose of quirky fun. Your family will be learning together, serving together, and laughing together each week—who doesn't want to make time for *that*?

So grab a parent, find the kids, and spend some time with the one best friend you all can share—the Bible.

Sheila Walsh

SPECIAL FEATURES

MEMORY VERSE

Each devo ties to a special scripture. Learn one verse each week, and they just might stick with you for a lifetime.

LET'S TALK

Get to talking and to knowing each other better with these fun discussion questions. Each week you'll find one question for parents and one question for kids. Who knows what you'll discover?

FAMILY FUN

Hi! I'm Charlie, and this is Wilson. Say hello, Wilson.

Mmmm, pizza.

You'll find an assortment of activities with something for each person in the family. Follow a scavenger hunt through Scripture in *Look for It*, grab the glue for *Crafty Creations*, let the performers in the family ham it up with *Act It Out*, and then enjoy a *Birdbrain Idea* or two for good measure.

WEEKLY CHALLENGE ?

Who doesn't love a good challenge? Each week your family can work together to take on something new—from service projects to Scripture memory to silly games. It's a great way to make memories and grow hearts at the same time.

BACK TO THE BIBLE

Each week's devo connects to a Bible story, so this feature tells you where to find the story behind the message. Open the Word, get to reading, and see what else there is to learn.

And here's something fun. . . . The spot art next to this feature will be part of the upcoming *The Bible Is Your Best Friend Bible Storybook*. So you have some search-and-find fun waiting for you soon!

✔ CHECKPOINT!

What message did you learn this week? Did you tackle the challenge? Keep track of your family's progress by checking the box!

CONTENTS

MEMORY VERSE

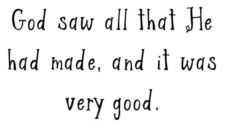

God saw all that He had made, and it was very good.

–Genesis 1:31

GOD MADE IT ALL

What are the biggest things you can think of? How about the tiniest? Do you know that God made all those amazing things–the big, the small, the magnificent, the microscopic–in just six days? Gigantic solar systems, tiny amoebas, and our amazing human bodies–God made it all from nothing. Read this week's memory verse, Genesis 1:31. After God made everything in just six days, He looked around and saw that it was all good. Everything was made by Him, and He made it perfectly perfect. Wow–that's one powerful God.

You and your family are also parts of God's creation, the best parts! He put you all together to love one another and to help each other learn more about Him. One way a family grows closer in love and nearer to God is by praying, worshipping, and studying the Bible together. The Bible is another wonderful thing that God created; He used people to write the words and put it all together exactly how He wanted it.

Even if you don't know a lot about the Bible right now, by the time we are finished, you will discover that the Bible is your very best friend. It is God's Word, His love story directly to us. It tells who God is, what He thinks, and the way He wants us to live. The Bible is one way God speaks to us, and it's the perfect way for us to get to know our wonderful Creator!

Ask your kids!

LET'S TALK

What is your favorite thing that God created?

Are there any things you wish God *didn't* create?

Ask your parents!

FAMILY FUN
LOOK FOR IT

The Bible is divided into sections called books. The first book is called Genesis. Read aloud Genesis, chapters 1 and 2:1–3. They tell us that God made everything in six days. See if you can discover which things God created on each of those six days.

Hey, God made us before He made people!

Dogs rule.

The books of the Bible are gathered into two parts: the Old Testament and the New Testament. The Old Testament tells about what happened up until the time when God's Son, Jesus, was born. The New Testament tells what happened after Jesus came into the world.

Split up into teams. See if your team can memorize and name all the books in the Bible. You have one week to do it. Ready? Set? Go!

Hint: There are 66 books, 39 in the Old Testament and 27 in the New Testament. Divide them among your team members to memorize. Older team members can help the younger ones.

WEEKLY CHALLENGE

Remember: You can find the Bible story of God's creation in Genesis 1 and 2:1–3.

✔
CHECKPOINT!
We did it! We memorized all 66 books of the Bible!

MEMORY VERSE

For all have sinned
and fall short of the
glory of God.

–Romans 3:23

SNEAKY SIN

Mark looked down at the big fat D on his math test. "I'm really disappointed with your grade," his teacher said. "Get your parents to sign your test, and we'll talk about it tomorrow."

Mark was not looking forward to talking to his parents. He knew he had to do it, but he also knew that they were worried about other things right now. His bad grade would only add to their stress. *Maybe it would be best just to sign my mom's name,* he thought. *Then she won't have to worry about my grades. Isn't making Mom happy the right thing to do?* Mark planned to lie; sin was sneaking up on him.

Sin is all the bad things we do when we ignore God's Word and His will for our lives. When sin comes into our hearts, our love for God begins to die. Sin likes to disguise itself as something good, something you really, really want. But what you want might not always be what is best for you. That is exactly what happened to Adam and Eve. A sneaky snake appeared dangling from a tree.

"Come on," it hissed. "Eat the fruit. If you do, you will be just like God. You will know everything there is to know about good and evil."

So Eve ate the fruit, and she gave some to Adam. And that's where sin found a place in people's hearts. Thousands of years later, sin is still sneaking up on us.

Thankfully, Mark realized that although lying about his grade seemed like the easier choice, it was a sin. He made the right choice and talked to his parents. Being honest was what God wanted Mark to do, and his parents were able to get him the help he needed in math.

What about you? Has sin sneaked up on you too? This week's memory verse tells us that we all sin and we all disappoint God. But God forgives us when we ask Him, and His Word–the Bible–can help us resist even the sneakiest of sins!

LET'S TALK

Can you think of some examples of how sin is sneaky?

Ask your kids!

What sin did you struggle with when you were my age?

Ask your parents!

FAMILY FUN

BIRDBRAIN IDEA

The leader stands across the room from the others with his or her back to them. When the leader says, "Go," the others (sneaky snakes) slither very slowly on their bellies toward the leader. At any time, the leader may turn around and say, "Stop!" Snakes must freeze in place. Any caught moving are out. Play until just one snake remains.

WEEKLY CHALLENGE

The Bible can help us recognize sin and fight it because it is filled with God's instructions. Read and discuss these Bible verses:

If you do what is right, won't you be accepted? But if you do not do what is right, sin is crouching at the door. Its desire is for you, but you must rule over it. –Genesis 4:7

No temptation has overtaken you except what is common to humanity. God is faithful, and He will not allow you to be tempted beyond what you are able, but with the temptation He will also provide a way of escape so that you are able to bear it. –1 Corinthians 10:13

God is called our heavenly Father, and like any good parent He knows best what is right for His children. Uncovering sin and saying no to it always makes Him happy.

This week, everyone think of at least one way to recognize sin and keep it from sneaking into your life. Then get together and share your ideas.

You can read more about how Adam and Eve gave in to sin by looking in the Bible in Genesis 2:4–3:24.

✓ **CHECKPOINT!**
We found some ways to say no to sin.

17

MEMORY VERSE

Fear God and keep
His commands,
because this is for
all humanity.

–Ecclesiastes 12:13

OBEY DAY-TO-DAY

We might think that the story of Noah's ark is mostly about a big floating zoo, but it's also a story about obedience. Noah obeyed God, but it wasn't easy—it took a lot of physical work, months and months of patience, and the ability to put up with a lot of stinky animals. But in the end, his obedience saved his family.

So, how does your obedience compare to Noah's? When your mom reminds you to clean your room, do you wait until you get around to it? When your dad asks you to help your little brother, do you do so with a smile or a complaint? When you read God's command in the Bible to love your enemies, do you wonder if you really have to obey that one?

Day-to-day obedience might not seem as important to us when it's not life or death as it was for Noah. But God still wants us to be obedient so that we will stay safe and grow into the kinds of people He planned for us to be. Obeying God is one way we show Him that we love Him and want to serve Him.

The Bible is clear about the importance of obedience. When we read this week's memory verse, Ecclesiastes 12:13, we see that God wants us to "keep His commands." What we don't see are any extra phrases about "when we get around to it," "while complaining," or "only if we think we *really* have to."

Maybe your obedience needs some tuning up. Think about all the good things that happen when you have the right attitude and obey God—you grow closer to Him, you set a better example for others, and you avoid disagreements with your families and friends. Those results are pretty great, and just think—they don't require you to spend any time stuck on a stinky ark. Obedience is definitely the right choice.

What do you think was the best part of being on the ark? How about the worst part?

Ask your kids!

When have you been obedient, even when it was hard?

Ask your parents!

FAMILY FUN

BIRDBRAIN IDEA

Work in teams. Each team writes this week's memory verse on a piece of paper and hides it. Give the other team a list of instructions to find it. For example: Go to the kitchen, turn left, take two steps right, turn around.... Which team can find the hidden verse in the shortest time?

WEEKLY CHALLENGE

NOAH →

ESTHER ←

CAMELS ←↓

Talk about obedience and why it's important. Do you think Noah had a hard time being obedient? Can you think of other people in the Bible who obeyed God? What about people your family knows? Think about men and women who are careful to do what God says, and are obedient. Then make a list of those people. They can be your "ready-to-obey role models." You can remember them when you are tempted to grumble or disobey.

Throughout the week, look for ways to obey quickly, fully, and with a smile. Look at your list if you need a role-model reminder.

Read more about Noah's obedience in the Bible: Genesis 6:5–9:17.

✓ **CHECKPOINT!**

We found ready-to-obey role models this week!

MEMORY VERSE

Now faith is the reality of what is hoped for, the proof of what is not seen.

–Hebrews 11:1

KEEP THE FAITH

All together now! Take a deep breath: *Innnnnnnnnn* . . . Now exhale slowly: *Ouuuuuuuuut* . . . Did you feel air fill up your lungs? Did you feel it leave you? You can't see air, but you know it exists because it keeps you alive. You can't see God either, but you feel Him with you like you feel air going in and out of your body.

Believing in something you can't see is called *faith*. Faith means trusting God not only to be with you but also to keep His promises.

Abraham trusted God when God said, "Look at the sky and count the stars. Your offspring will be that many." (*Offspring* means children and grandchildren.) Abraham wanted a family, and he had faith that God would provide what he asked for. It took a long time, but one day Abraham and his wife had a son, and later grandchildren, and then great-grandchildren. Abraham's family kept growing and growing, just like God promised.

This week's memory verse, Hebrews 11:1, reminds you that although you can't see what's up ahead, God can. He hears your prayers, and He knows exactly what you need.

Faith isn't always easy because we want what we hope for right away. But God doesn't work like that. Often He tells us to wait. Waiting builds our faith and trust in Him. Faith helps us feel safe and secure with God while we wait for what we hope for. If we have faith in His love for us, then we know for sure that God is with us every minute of every day because we feel Him in our hearts. And faith pleases God. It shows how much we love Him, and it proves we believe that He can do anything.

The Bible is a great big story about God doing exactly what He says. Read it, and you will discover that the Bible is God's story, written for you, a story about hope and faith.

What is something you've asked God for?

Ask your kids!

Do you ever find it hard to have faith in God?

Ask your parents!

FAMILY FUN

LOOK FOR IT

Look, I think I see the Dog Star.

Go outside with your family on a starry night and take a good look at the sky. Can you find the Big Dipper and the Little Dipper?

If clouds came along right now and covered up the stars, would the stars still be there behind the clouds?

Remember: Faith means believing in what you cannot see.

Are you Sirius?

24

Make a simple obstacle course using things you have around the house. Think of it as a maze that you need to go through to get from Point A to Point B.

Work in pairs. One person is the leader. The other promises to be led through the course with their eyes covered. (No peeking!)

It takes faith to allow someone to lead you along a mixed-up path, doesn't it? But a good leader leads you safely through. That's the sort of leader God is. You can't see Him, but you can have faith that He is with you, leading the way you should go.

Read more about God's promise to Abraham in Genesis 15:1-6; 21:1-2.

✔

CHECKPOINT!
We learned what it means to have faith in God.

MEMORY VERSE

Love the LORD your
God with all your
heart, with all your
soul, and with all
your strength.

—Deuteronomy 6:5

LOVE CONNECTION

Emily's little brother, Peter, liked playing checkers, and Emily did too. Sometimes she warned Peter if he was about to make a bad move. "Are you sure you want to move there?" Or she might say, "Uh-oh" and let Peter rethink his move. Emily enjoyed helping her little brother because she loved him.

When Peter thought that Emily wasn't looking, he moved one of her checkers so he could jump it. Emily saw. "Why did you do that?" she asked. It made her sad that her brother cheated, especially since she had been so helpful and loving. Peter hadn't thought about Emily's feelings at all. He just wanted to win. He knew cheating was wrong, but he did it anyway.

Have you ever wanted something so much that you didn't care what you did to get it? The Bible tells about a boy named Esau who traded all of God's blessings for a bowl of hot stew. He wasn't starving. He didn't really need that stew. But just then, at that very moment, Esau wanted stew more than anything else. He didn't stop to think about trading God's love for something to eat.

Deuteronomy 6:5 reminds us to love God with all of our hearts, souls, and strength. That means loving God more than anything else. What if someone said to you that eating dinner or winning a game was more important than loving you? When Esau traded God's blessings for stew and when Peter cheated, it was just like saying to God, "I love what I want more than I love You."

Love is more than words or a feeling. We show our love through the ways we act. One way to show God some love is by doing what's right. The Bible can help you with that. The more you learn about God's love for you, the more you will want to love God back.

LET'S TALK

What are some ways to show God you love Him?

Ask your kids!

Who do you love, other than God?

Ask your parents!

FAMILY FUN

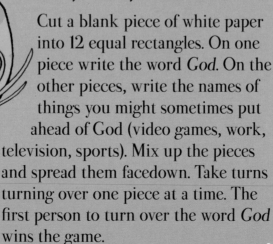

BIRDBRAIN IDEA

Cut a blank piece of white paper into 12 equal rectangles. On one piece write the word *God*. On the other pieces, write the names of things you might sometimes put ahead of God (video games, work, television, sports). Mix up the pieces and spread them facedown. Take turns turning over one piece at a time. The first person to turn over the word *God* wins the game.

WEEKLY CHALLENGE

Wanna sit here?

This week, love God by spending time praying or reading the Bible instead of doing what you want. Another way to love God is by putting the feelings of others ahead of your own. Maybe you want to sit with your friends, but you notice a new kid sitting alone. What do you think you should do? What will make God happy? Try your best to show God some love by always doing what's right. At the end of this week, get together with your family and talk about the ways you showed God you love Him.

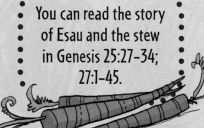

You can read the story of Esau and the stew in Genesis 25:27-34; 27:1-45.

✔ CHECKPOINT!

We practiced loving God more than anything else.

MEMORY VERSE

We know that all things work together for the good of those who love God: those who are called according to His purpose.

–Romans 8:28

IT'S ALL GOOD

I'm having a bad day." Everyone says that sometimes. A bad day can be a little bad, like a bee sting, or really bad, like a big wind that blows you down the sidewalk and leaves you feeling out of control.

Do you wonder: *If God can fix anything, then why do bad things happen?* People have wondered about that forever, and the truth is only God knows the answer.

This week's memory verse, Romans 8:28, says: "We know that all things work together for the good of those who love God: those who are called according to His purpose." It means that God can take a big, smelly, broken mess, pick up all the pieces, and make them into something new. He may not put the pieces together in the way that you expect, but however it ends up, it will all be for good. Everything God does is good.

When Jackson's dad got a new job in another state, it meant moving across the country. Moving was the last thing Jackson wanted. The idea of leaving his friends, his house, and his school made him cry. "I don't get it, God," he prayed. "You know that I don't want to move, but I guess that's what You want. So please work it all out and help me not to feel worried or sad." Did you notice that Jackson didn't complain or run away from God? Instead, he trusted God to turn his mess into something good. And that is exactly what God did. In only a few months, Jackson felt comfortable in his new house and school.

You can always trust God to untangle a mess. And while God is working, the Bible will help. God's Word gives you hope when your world is upside down. It also helps calm your bad feelings. If you are worried about doing something new or about anything else, God is with you, and so is the Bible– both are your friends in bad times and good.

What is the messiest mess you can think of?

Ask your kids!

What helps you feel better when you have a bad day?

Ask your parents!

FAMILY FUN

CRAFTY CREATION

On a large piece of paper write the words ALL THINGS WORK TOGETHER FOR THE GOOD OF THOSE WHO LOVE GOD. Use your crayons to make pretty designs all over the paper. Now cut the paper into puzzle pieces and ask another family member to put it back together.

Often God uses people to help Him clean up a mess. Maybe you will turn on the evening news and see people helping each other after a storm, or you might read about people providing food or clothing for someone in need. In your neighborhood, community, and all over the world, God uses people to help Him work bad things into something good.

This week, see if you can come up with five ways that your family can help people in need. Then act on one of your ideas.

Read a Bible story about God turning Joseph's situation around for good in Genesis 37:1-36; 39:1–41:57.

✔
CHECKPOINT!
We learned that God is good all the time, and whatever He does is good.

33

MEMORY VERSE

"Remember, I am with you always, to the end of the age."

—Matthew 28:20

FOREVER AND ALWAYS

God is like the wind. He is all around you all the time. You might not notice Him, and then, like a small breeze, you sense His presence when He helps you with something like answering a little prayer or reminding you to do something good. Other times God comes whooshing into your life like a big wind that almost knocks you off your feet. He does something grand, something you never even imagined. That's God's way of reminding you He is right there with you, big and powerful, loving you all the time.

God knew you even before you were born, and He will be with you every day of your life, forever and always. God has no beginning and no end. He has always been and He always will be. That's an amazing idea, isn't it?

Imagine if you could see what everything on earth is doing right this very minute. Every person. Every animal. And not only see them, but also be in control of everything that happens everywhere, always working it out for good. That's who God is. Well, God is even bigger than that! He doesn't even have to see everything to know what is going on. He knew everything that was ever going to happen and how He would use it for good before He even created the world! That's who God is.

This week's memory verse is God speaking directly to you. It begins with the important word *remember*. God wants you to remember He is with you all the time. When you get up in the morning, God is there. Everywhere you go, He is with you. He sees and hears you all the time. God is there when you go to bed at night and while you sleep.

Don't think that He is spying on you or waiting to see if you do something wrong. God is with you all the time because He loves you. He is always there helping you and protecting you from that sneaky old thing called sin.

Forever is a very long time, too long to be measured. It has no end. That's what God is—forever—and so are His words in your best friend, the Bible.

What do you not like about God being everywhere?

Ask your kids!

How would you describe forever?

Ask your parents!

FAMILY FUN
LOOK FOR IT

Use these clues to find another Scripture verse in the Bible about God being with you: Look for the 23rd book in the Old Testament. Find the chapter that comes just before chapter 42. Count your fingers, then find the verse equal to the number of your fingers. Now read that verse aloud.

But dogs don't have fingers!

I guess we'll have to count on our toes.

WEEKLY CHALLENGE

God promises to help you and give you strength. He tells you never to be afraid because He is with you. Your challenge this week is to look for clues that God is with you all of the time. Think of yourselves as detectives. Work alone or in teams to see how many ways you can find to prove that God is all around you. Then get together and talk about it. Who found the most clues? Who found the most unusual clue?

Say a prayer together and thank God for His presence in your life.

Read about God being with Joseph in Genesis 41:53–46:34; 50:15–21.

✔

CHECKPOINT!
We know for sure that God is with us now and forever.

MEMORY VERSE

I will praise You
because I have been
remarkably and
wonderfully made.

−Psalm 139:14

WONDERFUL, REMARKABLE YOU

God makes every living thing, even silly-looking things with strange names like Dumbo octopuses, proboscis monkeys, and aye-ayes. God creates everything and gives it a purpose.

God created the people whose stories are in the Bible. Their purpose is to teach you about God. For example, Noah's story is about faith. Daniel's story is about trust; Jonah's is about obedience. And Jesus' story—the most important of all—is about forgiveness and mercy.

God makes some people with the purpose of serving Him as missionaries and pastors. He creates others to be helpers. God gives some people special talents and makes others role models. And a few people, sadly, turn away from God, and their purpose is to teach us what *not* to do.

God planned your whole life before you were born. He knew what you would look like from the top of your head to the tips of your toes and even how many hairs would grow on your head. Everything you will ever say and everything you will do, all the days of your life, are part of His plan.

Psalm 139:14 reminds us that we are remarkably and wonderfully made. That means you! You are God's creation: perfect, wonderful, remarkable, and one-of-a-kind. There never has been and never will be another you. So be the best that you can be. You might not know what your purpose is, but God knows. You are here for a reason. You are part of His plan.

There are three things that you can do right now while you wait for God to reveal your purpose. Read the Bible and learn from it. Keep God's commands. And tell others about Him.

In His own time, God might use you to do something great. Pray and ask Him to show you what to do. He loves you, and He will guide you. And remember to praise Him! Give God thanks for making wonderful, remarkable you.

LET'S TALK

What makes you special?

Ask your kids!

Do you know your purpose?

Ask your parents!

FAMILY FUN

BIRDBRAIN IDEA

Find a small mirror to use for this activity. Everyone sit in a circle. The first person looks into the mirror and says, "I am wonderful because . . ." and adds one way that God made them special. Pass the mirror to the next person who does the same thing. Keep passing the mirror until everyone has had several turns.

Mom, you are the best cook in the world!

And you are the smartest girl in the world!

When you give someone a compliment, you remind them that you see one of the wonderful ways that God made them. You might say things like, "I love it that you are always so willing to help," or "Your laugh makes me feel happy," or "You are a beautiful dancer."

This week, make it a priority to compliment each other. At the end of the week, get together and discuss the ways in which each family member helps to make your family special. Then give God some praise for putting you together and making your family remarkably and wonderfully His.

God made Moses to do great things. Read about him in Exodus 1:6–2:10, 23–25; 3:1–4:20.

✔ CHECKPOINT!

We discovered many ways that God made us special.

■

MEMORY VERSE

"For I know the plans
I have for you"—this is
the Lord's declaration—
"plans for your welfare,
not for disaster, to give
you a future and a hope."

—Jeremiah 29:11

YES, YOU CAN!

Hannah sang in the children's choir at church. She loved singing. But Hannah only felt comfortable singing with others. If she sang alone and anyone heard, Hannah got butterflies in her stomach. She worried, *What if people say that I have a lovely voice just to make me feel good? What if I have a terrible voice? What if I sing and everyone laughs and makes fun of me?* All of those what-ifs whipped Hannah into such a state that when the choir director chose her to sing a solo in church, Hannah felt like throwing up. That little voice inside screamed, "It's too hard. You can't do it. Say no." But Hannah couldn't say no to her choir director. Then everyone really would laugh.

God had given Hannah a beautiful singing voice, and He wanted her to use it. Hearing her sing pleased Him. And that snarky little voice inside? It wasn't His. God wanted Hannah to share her gift with others.

This week's memory verse, Jeremiah 29:11, speaks God's words: "For I know the plans I have for you, plans for your welfare, not for disaster, to give you a future and a hope." It reminds us that God is in control.

God had planned for Hannah to sing a solo in church. And Hannah did sing! God gave her all the courage she needed, and when she started to sing, all of her fear melted away. The solo was not a disaster as she worried it might be; it was a huge success.

Have you felt like Hannah? Maybe you had the opportunity to do something great, but that little voice inside said, "This is too hard for you," or "You're not good enough, strong enough, or smart enough."

Don't listen to that voice! Read your Bible and find out what God says. He is in control, and He will provide everything you need to carry out His plans. Trust Him to turn your "No, I can't" into a big "Yes! I can."

What is something you do very well?

Ask your kids!

Was there a time when you thought you couldn't do something, but did it?

Ask your parents!

FAMILY FUN

ACT IT OUT

Get together as a family and act out Hannah's story. Show how God changed Hannah's "No, I can't" into a "Yes, I can." Perform your skit for an audience of family members or friends. Whenever your Hannah says, "No, I can't," have the audience answer, "Yes, you can!"

WEEKLY CHALLENGE

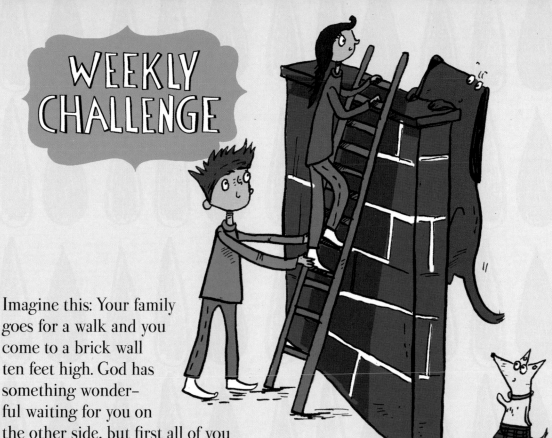

Imagine this: Your family goes for a walk and you come to a brick wall ten feet high. God has something wonderful waiting for you on the other side, but first all of you must get over that wall. You have no ladder or tools. There are no trees nearby. You must rely on each other for help. Your challenge is to decide how to get over the wall.

Remember: The enemy, Satan, puts obstacles in your way, trying to discourage you from carrying out God's plans. But God is in control. He always finds ways to complete His plans.

God tells Moses about His plan in Exodus 7:2–5.

✔ CHECKPOINT!
We know that God is in control, and His plans are always good.

MEMORY VERSE

"If you love Me,
you will keep
My commands."

–John 14:15

TEN IMPORTANT RULES

We often call God "Father" because He is the Great Father of all. Like every good father, God makes rules for His children. His rules help people stay out of trouble.

Long ago, God chose Moses to be a great leader. God gave Moses two stone tablets on which He had written His rules for all of us. The Bible calls them the Ten Commandments.

Number one is to always put God first, to put Him before sports, TV, playing games, and everything else.

The second is to worship God only. You should never love someone or something so much that it becomes as important as God.

Third: Watch your language. Whenever you say God's name or speak about Him, it should be with great respect.

Fourth: Take Sunday off to worship and honor God.

Fifth: Respect your parents.

Sixth: Don't hurt anyone.

The seventh commandment is for married people: Be faithful to each other.

Eighth: Don't steal.

Ninth: Don't lie.

Tenth: Don't want what others have.

God gave us these rules because He loves us. Following them shows God that we love Him. But nobody is able to keep all the rules all the time. That's because no one but God is perfect.

Your job is to love God with all your heart, with all your soul, and with all your mind and to do your very best to follow the rules. When you put God first, you will usually do what is right. Sometimes, though, you will mess up. When you do, pray to God and tell Him about it. He will surely forgive you because Jesus paid for your sins on the cross.

Why do you think it is good to have rules?

Ask your kids!

Which commandment do you find hardest to follow?

Ask your parents!

FAMILY FUN

CRAFTY CREATION

Make a large poster listing the Ten Commandments. Decorate it with pretty art. While you work, talk about what each commandment means. Then put the poster someplace where your family will see it every day. (The kitchen and bathroom are good places, or by a door you use most often.)

WEEKLY CHALLENGE

This week's challenge has two parts. The first is for everyone in the family to memorize the Ten Commandments. The second part is to show God some love by trying to obey ALL of His commandments all week long. See if you can do it. Can anyone in your family go through the whole week without breaking one of God's commands?

Talk about rules. Do parents make rules because they love their children? Why is it some-times hard to follow rules? End by thanking God for giving us rules, and remember to tell Him you love Him.

You can find the Ten Commandments in your Bible in Exodus 20:1–17.

THE COMMANDMENTS
X
I.
II.

CHECKPOINT!
We did it! We memorized the Ten Commandments.

MEMORY VERSE

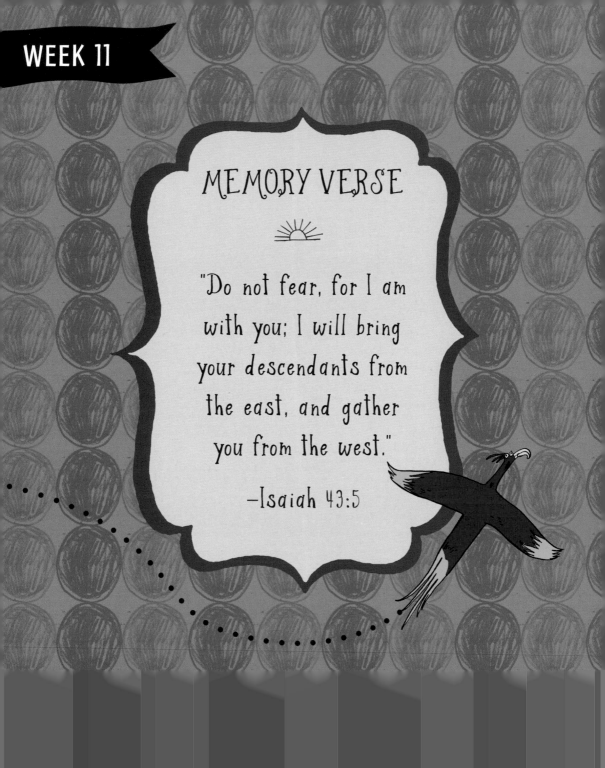

"Do not fear, for I am with you; I will bring your descendants from the east, and gather you from the west."

–Isaiah 43:5

BE BRAVE

What are you afraid of? Many people are afraid of creepy, crawly bugs. Some people are afraid of thunder and lightning. Others find made-up things, like monsters, scary. A few people are even afraid of being afraid. The silly-sounding word for that is *phobophobia*. If you are afraid of absolutely everything, well, that is called *panophobia*, and that would be just awful!

Fear is not a nice feeling. Sometimes it strikes fast and hard. Other times it builds up slowly. Fear likes to make its home inside the hearts of people, and that's not good because the heart is where God wants to live.

In the Bible, God says, "Do not fear, for I am with you." Many times He tells His people not to be frightened; still, some find it hard to trust Him in scary times. Instead of being brave and facing their fears head-on, they run and try to hide, even from God. They allow fear to be like a big bully that makes them feel weak and small.

Think of the bravest people you know. What if firefighters were too afraid to fight a fire? Buildings would burn to the ground. What if police officers were too afraid to go after the bad guys? The bad guys would rule. What if people were too afraid to tell others about God? How would they hear that God loves them?

Do you believe that God is stronger than anything you are afraid of? He is! He doesn't like it when fear creeps into your heart. And because God loves you, He will certainly help when you are afraid.

The Bible teaches us that trusting God is so important. Whenever you feel scared, trust Him to make you brave. Whether you fear a visit to the doctor's office, a problem at school, a creepy, crawly bug, or a thunderstorm, God is right there with you. He is able to squash anything that you are afraid of—anything at all.

What are you most afraid of?

Ask your kids!

Were you afraid of anything when you were a kid?

Ask your parents!

FAMILY FUN

BIRDBRAIN IDEA

Get together and tell a silly, scary add-on story. Someone begins the made-up story and ends at a scary part. Before the story continues, everyone says, "But God said, 'Do not be afraid.'" Then the next person continues the story, also stopping at a scary part. Everyone says, "But God said, 'Do not be afraid.'" Keep going until someone ends the story.

WEEKLY CHALLENGE

Nobody has to face fear alone. That is one reason why God puts us in families. We help each other to be brave.

This week, discuss some of the things that each family member is afraid of. Then come up with ways the whole family can help with those fears. Telling someone that you are afraid is the first step. The next is knowing that God and others will always be there to help. You might want to use a buddy system. Assign each family member a buddy whom they can go to for help whenever they feel afraid.

Read about two men, Joshua and Caleb, who stood up to fear in Numbers 13:1–14:38.

CHECKPOINT!

We trust God to help us when we feel afraid.

MEMORY VERSE

I have treasured Your word in my heart so that I may not sin against You.

–Psalm 119:11

WORTH MORE THAN SILVER AND GOLD

The Bible is sometimes called the Word of God. Do you know why? Because all the words written in the Bible came from Him. God used men to write the words down, but the message is God's.

When you open your Bible, you find God's instructions about how to live in a way that pleases Him. More than a book of rules, it's God's love letter to us. The Bible helps us when we are afraid, sick, tired, or lonely. It lets us know God's promises to us, encourages us, and even provides glimpses into the future. Most importantly, the Bible tells us what we must do to be saved from our sins.

God's words in the Bible are priceless. Nothing else is as valuable and important. Imagine gathering up all the world's silver and gold, all its money, jewelry, expensive houses, cars, and every other valuable thing you can think of. What would it all cost? Well, no one could buy it anyway because there would be nothing left to buy it with! No matter what value we might place on all the wealth in the world, it would never come close to God's Word. The Bible is worth more than everything.

One of the reasons the Bible is priceless is because everything in it is true–every book, chapter, verse, and story. There aren't any myths in the Bible. When you read Bible stories like Noah's ark, Jonah and the big fish, or Daniel staying safe in the lions' den, all of it is true. The Bible is filled with true stories about the great things God does.

The Bible is also priceless because it teaches us who God is, and it tells us about Jesus, God's Son, and how He provides our way to heaven. Getting to know Jesus is the most priceless gift of all.

Get in the habit of reading your Bible every day. God wrote it for you, and it is one way that He talks to you. When you read the Bible, you can store God's Word in your heart and treasure it. Make it worth more than silver and gold.

What one thing do you treasure the most?

Ask your kids!

What do you do if you find some parts of the Bible hard to understand?

Ask your parents!

FAMILY FUN

LOOK FOR IT

The Bible describes God's Word as sharp like a _____.
Let's find a Scripture that will help us fill in the blank!

- First, look in your Bible for the only book in the New Testament that starts with the letter *H*.
- Then find the chapter that equals $2 + 2$.
- Now read the verse that equals one dozen.

What is the word that goes in the blank above?

En Garde.

Touché.

WEEKLY CHALLENGE

At the beginning of the week, draw a big heart on a piece of paper and label it MY HEART. Next, choose one person to hide twenty-five pennies around the house. The rest of the family looks for the pennies throughout the week. Each time someone finds a penny, that person should place it inside the heart.

After all the pennies have been found, talk about how valuable the Bible is in your everyday life and why it is important to memorize its verses and store them in your hearts. Remember: Nothing is more valuable than God's Word.

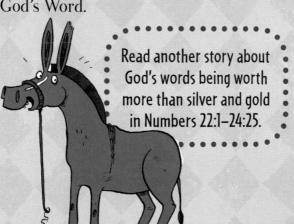

Read another story about God's words being worth more than silver and gold in Numbers 22:1–24:25.

✔ CHECKPOINT!

We learned that God's words are priceless.

MEMORY VERSE

For we walk by faith,
not by sight.

—2 Corinthians 5:7

A BIG PROBLEM

William had a problem: a kid in his class named Everett. Every day at recess, Everett picked on Will. He called Will names, shoved him, and made fun of him. Everett was a big–and I mean *big*–bully, and the very sight of him made Will shake. *What am I going to do?* Will worried. *He's too big to fight. If I tell on him, that might make things worse.* Will didn't know what to do.

One night Will prayed and asked God for help. Then after praying, he decided to tell his parents about Everett.

"Let's try this," his mom said. "In the classroom tomorrow, find a time when you can talk quietly with Everett. Ask if you two can be friends instead of fight. If that doesn't work, we'll ask your teacher and principal to help."

It made Will's stomach flip-flop just thinking of walking up to Everett and asking to be friends. But Will knew in his heart it was the right thing to do.

The next morning, in the classroom before class started, Will walked up to Everett and said, "I really want to like you. So let's be friends and not fight." And do you know what? It worked! Will and Everett became buddies.

Second Corinthians 5:7 reminds us that God sometimes leads people in ways they don't expect. We don't know what God will do, but He wants us to remember that He has everything under control.

When something troubles you and you don't know what to do, stand tall, trust God, and have faith that He will lead you in the right direction. Start by doing what you know is right–read the Bible, pray, and ask God for help. Keep praying, doing what is right, and having faith that God will lead you. In time, He will solve your problem, just like He did Will's. God is indeed great and mighty, and He can solve any problem at all, including yours.

Do you have a problem that's troubling you?

Did you ever have to stand up to a bully?

Ask your kids!

Ask your parents!

FAMILY FUN

BIRDBRAIN IDEA

Give each person a brown paper bag, and ask them to hide something good inside. Now mix up all the bags and put them in a row. Try to guess what is in each one. You can't see what is inside, but you know it's something good because you trust the person who filled the bag. That's how faith works. Did anyone guess correctly what was in all of the bags?

WEEKLY CHALLENGE

Get together and talk about different situations in which people have faith and do what is right even when they aren't sure what will happen. For example: Firefighters and police officers don't know what will happen when they answer a call, but that does not stop them from helping; a mountain climber doesn't know for sure whether he will reach the mountaintop, but that does not keep him from trying. How many more examples can you come up with?

See if each family member can tell about one time when they acted in faith without knowing the outcome. Then give God praise and thank Him for solving your problems.

For another story about faith, read Joshua 1:1, 3-4.

CHECKPOINT!
We have faith God will help us when we don't know what to do.

MEMORY VERSE

I am able to do all
things through Him
who strengthens me.

–Philippians 4:13

IT WILL ALL BE OKAY

Are you strong enough to lift a glass of milk? How about a gallon of milk? How about a crate filled with gallons of milk? Could you lift the cow that gave the milk? That's a funny idea, isn't it? But if you think about it, it's possible for a person to lift a cow if they get other people to help. Humans can find the strength to do almost anything with a little help from their friends.

Some people are physically strong and can lift big things, but people are also spiritually strong. That means their faith in God helps them do what they think is impossible. Addie's story is one example. When she found out that her parents were getting a divorce, she was heartbroken. She wondered why her parents were splitting up and how often she would see her dad after he moved out. Addie worried about where she would live and whether both parents would still love her. She even worried that maybe, somehow, she was to blame (of course, that wasn't true at all).

Addie prayed and asked God for help. She had faith that He would help her be brave and stay calm. Addie was reminded that both parents loved her and that God loved her too. With Him in control, everything would be okay.

This week's memory verse reminds us that God gives us strength to do what we might think is impossible. As you read the Bible and discover the amazing things God has helped people do, your trust in Him will grow. And as your trust grows, you will learn that God can give you the strength to accomplish even the most difficult things. After all, He is stronger than any challenge you might face!

Do you have a problem? God will help you solve it. Do you dream of doing something great? God will give you strength to work toward your dreams.

Remember: All things are possible with a little help from your best friend—the Bible—and a lot of help from God.

LET'S TALK

Do you have a big dream God can help you with?

Ask your kids!

What's the hardest thing you've ever done?

Ask your parents!

FAMILY FUN

BIRDBRAIN IDEA

Maybe you want to be a missionary someday and tell the world about God, or maybe you want to help save the whales or fight forest fires. Draw a picture of yourself doing something you dream about. Write this week's memory verse on your picture. Then put it in your room to remember that God gives you strength to do amazing things.

God helped Joshua do the impossible in Joshua 2:6.

Everyone stand up. Raise your arms up into the air. Stay that way, arms up high, for as long as you possibly can. When someone's arms grow so tired that he can't hold them up anymore, he should say, "I need a little help, please." Then the rest of you put down your arms and go help that person hold up his.

Now take a few minutes to read aloud Exodus 17:8–13.

God is stronger than the strongest army. When you are weak, God gives you strength. And remember this: You can count on help from your family and friends.

✔ CHECKPOINT!

We discovered that God gives us strength to do great things.

MEMORY VERSE

Trust in the LORD
with all your heart,
and do not rely on your
own understanding.

–Proverbs 3:5

THE SMALLEST AND YOUNGEST

If you are the smallest or youngest person in your family, maybe you think you are also the weakest. But that's not true! With God's help, even the smallest or youngest can do great things. As you read the Bible, you will discover stories about young people whom God used to carry out His plans.

Miriam, Moses' sister, played a part in saving his life when he was just a baby. If she hadn't, Moses wouldn't have become the great leader who gave us God's Ten Commandments. A boy named Samuel listened when God spoke to him and gave him little peeks into the future. Samuel didn't understand why God chose him, but Samuel's purpose was to warn people about things to come. When Joseph's big brothers sold him into slavery, they had no idea it was the beginning of God's plan to save a whole nation from starving. And a little boy who came to hear Jesus speak to a crowd of thousands had no idea that his small lunch would feed all those people. Did you notice that none of these young people knew that God was using them? Still, each was a piece in God's puzzle, His big plan for the world. Miriam, Moses, Samuel, Joseph, and the little boy with the lunch all had a purpose.

God has a purpose for you too. He brought you into the world for a reason. You might never understand how your piece fits into His big puzzle, but it does. God knows who you are and how He plans to use you.

You don't have to do anything at all to help God figure out His plan. He already knows. Your job is to obey what the Bible says in Proverbs 3:5–6: "Trust in the LORD with all your heart, and do not rely on your own understanding; think about Him in all your ways, and He will guide you on the right paths."

Ask your kids!

LET'S TALK

Do you think that God loves kids? Why?

Do you ever find it hard to just trust God?

Ask your parents!

FAMILY FUN

LOOK FOR IT

What will happen if you trust God in all that you do? Use these clues to find the Scripture with the answer:

- The verse is found in the twentieth book of the Bible.
- One foot plus four inches = _____ inches. (That's your chapter number!)
- Which number backward looks like an *E*? (That's your verse number!)

I found it!

I smell success!

WEEKLY CHALLENGE

Split up into two teams, and create a simple message using a code that you make up. You might use numbers, symbols, or even pictures for your message. The idea is to see if the other team can figure out what your message says.

How long did it take to figure out the other team's code?

You could spend a lifetime trying to figure out God's plans for you, but you may never see all the ways your life is being used. The Bible says to trust in Him with all your heart, and He will do the rest. Remember Miriam, Moses, Samuel, and Joseph? God was using them even when they couldn't see it! Keep trusting God to lead you, even when you don't understand, and you'll see that He can use you in amazing ways.

Read about another boy who was the smallest and youngest in Judges 6-8.

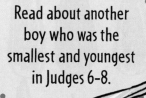

CHECKPOINT!

Every day we are learning to trust God more.

MEMORY VERSE

For everyone who calls
on the name of the
Lord will be saved.

–Romans 10:13

WHAT A MESS!

When you read your Bible, you will discover that God spends a good deal of time saving people—usually saving them from themselves. Humans aren't perfect, and they mess up. A lot.

Zoe asked her mom if she could take their new dog outside to play.

"Yes," Mom said. "But keep an eye on Boomer so he won't get into trouble."

Boomer was just a puppy. He knocked things over, broke them, and spilled them. Boomer often made a mess.

Zoe and Boomer played outside, and then Zoe's best friend, Annie, came over. After a while, they got bored with Boomer. Zoe allowed him to run around the yard wherever he wanted while the girls swung on Zoe's swing.

Well—you guessed it—what a mess! Boomer used those big, strong puppy paws to dig. And by the time Zoe noticed, Boomer had dug up her mom's flower garden and made gigantic holes in the lawn.

"I am so in trouble!" Zoe said.

What would you do if you were Zoe? She did the right thing. Zoe went inside and explained to her mom what happened. Her mother didn't like it that Zoe had messed up, but she forgave her because that is what parents do; they forgive their kids. Zoe and her mom cleaned up the mess together and told Boomer that his gardening days were over!

God is the best kind of parent. Your heavenly Father will always forgive you when you come to Him and say, "I'm sorry." And when you get into trouble, if you say, "God, help me," He will.

Forgiveness is a big part of God's plan. He knows that humans mess up. That's why God sent us His Son, Jesus. As you read the Bible, you will learn that Jesus saves people from sin. Whenever you mess up, remember: it is never too late to pray and ask God to forgive you. He will forgive you, help you, and save you.

LET'S TALK

Have you ever done something wrong and asked God to forgive you?

Ask your kids!

Will you always forgive me when I do something wrong?

Ask your parents!

FAMILY FUN

ACT IT OUT

Choose one of the song titles below. Then spend some family time creating lyrics and a melody for the song. You can make your song serious or fun.

- "God, I'm Sorry"
- "Dear God, Save Me"
- "The Forgiveness Rap"

All together now: Let's sing!

SORRY.

Everyone messes up sometimes. It just means that you are human, and it's never too late to say, "I'm sorry." This week, talk about why it is important to repent–to apologize to God for the bad things you do. Repentance means more than saying, "I'm sorry, God." It means changing your mind about what you have done and trying harder to please Him.

Create a forgiveness plan for your family. Make it comfortable for everyone to admit their mistakes. Promise to listen to each other, be understanding, and forgive.

A man named Samson messes up in Judges 13–16. Read about what he did.

CHECKPOINT!
We learned that God will always forgive us.

73

MEMORY VERSE

There is a friend
who stays closer
than a brother.

—Proverbs 18:24

YOUR PERFECT FRIEND FOREVER

The Bible has some great friendship stories: David and Jonathan, Elijah and Elisha, Ruth and Naomi. . . . Ruth and Naomi were such BFFs that Ruth promised never to leave Naomi. She said, "Wherever you go, I will go, and wherever you live, I will live; your people will be my people, and your God will be my God" (Ruth 1:16). She promised to stay with Naomi all the days of her life. Wow, that's a true friend.

Are you careful about choosing your friends? You should be. A good friend will never lead you into trouble.

Artie had just started in a new school, and the first kid he met was Jack. "Hey," Jack said. "Let's go to the store after school and steal some candy."

Steal? Artie knew that was wrong. He wanted more than anything to make friends in his new school, but God's voice inside him said, "Don't do it!" Artie made the right choice and said no. He and Jack never did become friends. But that was okay. Artie made plenty of new friends who trusted God just like he did.

Do you have a best friend? You do if you have a Bible. The Bible is a best friend because it tells us all about Jesus and why we need Him.

The Bible is also our friend because it is how God tells us about Himself. God is the perfect Friend. He is always loyal and faithful. You can trust Him to guide you in everything you do, and He will never leave you. God can do what no human friend can. He knows your thoughts and gives you everything you need. He is with you even when you are all alone. And God will not only be with you all the days of your life but also forever in heaven. When you make God your PFF (Perfect Friend Forever), nothing can ever separate you from Him, nothing at all.

Do your friends know about God? He wants to be their PFF too.

Ask your kids!

What is most important to you when choosing a best friend?

Who is your best friend, and how did you meet?

Ask your parents!

FAMILY FUN

BIRDBRAIN IDEA

Ruth said, "Wherever you go, I will go." Play this game with your family. Stand in a line and join hands. Spend the next fifteen minutes with everyone going and doing whatever they want, but *keep holding hands!*

Did it work, or did you all try to pull each other in different directions? Who got to choose which way you would go? Best friends often make the needs of the other person more important than their own.

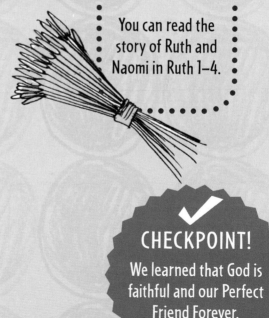

You can read the story of Ruth and Naomi in Ruth 1–4.

A guide is someone who shows you the way. A guide might take you through a state park, a museum, or a factory where things are made. God is a friend who always guides you. He leads you through your life and shows you the best way to go.

This week, each family member should think about where they would like God to take them. Have you dreamed of going someplace special, learning something new, or reaching an amazing goal? At the end of this week, get together and share your ideas. Where would you like to go with God?

✔ CHECKPOINT!

We learned that God is faithful and our Perfect Friend Forever.

MEMORY VERSE

God has chosen you
for salvation through
sanctification by the
Spirit and through
belief in the truth.

–2 Thessalonians 2:13

HERE I AM

God is so amazing that He knows the name of every person who is alive today or has ever lived or will live in the future.

Names are important to God. Did you know that God told some parents what to name their kids before they were born? That's how Ishmael, Isaac, Solomon, Josiah, John the Baptist, and Jesus got their names. And God renamed some people too. He changed Abram's name to Abraham. He gave Jacob the new name Israel, and God changed Saul's name to Paul.

When you read your Bible, you will discover stories where God spoke aloud to people and called them by name. Abraham, Jacob, Moses, and Samuel all heard God call their names, and they answered, "Here I am!"

God knows your name too. He *chose* you to be His child. He didn't give you your name, like He did some people in the Bible, but God knew what your parents would name you even before they did. God knows everything.

God calls on every grown-up and kid to follow Him. He wants them to be His family, and He wants them all saved from sneaky sin. Faith is a gift from God that He chooses to give us. But when we believe, we still need to choose to follow God.

We follow God and become His children by believing in His Son, Jesus, and trusting that Jesus will take us to heaven someday. The Bible tells us that Jesus is the only way to get there. And the Bible also says that our names are written in a book in heaven.

You probably won't hear God speak your name aloud while you're here on earth. But you need to believe by faith that He knows who you are and wants more than anything for you to love and obey Him. Someday God may choose you to do something great. If He calls on you, then you will be ready. Just like Abraham, Jacob, Moses, and Samuel, you can stand up and say, "God, here I am!"

LET'S TALK

If you have kids someday, what will you name them?

Ask your kids!

How did you choose my name?

Ask your parents!

FAMILY FUN

CRAFTY CREATION

Using paper, crayons, and scissors, make some bookmarks for your Bible. Write on each bookmark "Here I am, God," and decorate them with cool designs and pictures. You can use the bookmarks to mark your weekly memory verses in your Bible.

WEEKLY CHALLENGE

This week, make a little gift for each person in your family, something simple like a picture you draw or a small treat. At the end of the week, get together and give each other your gifts one at a time. When giving the gift, say, "I chose this for you."

God chose all of you to be His children and to offer you the gift of salvation (to be saved from sin). Talk about why it is important to follow God. What does it mean to live with Him forever in heaven? Along with salvation, what are some other gifts God has given you?

A boy named Samuel heard God call his name. Read about it in 1 Samuel 1–3.

✔ CHECKPOINT!

We learned that God chose each of us, and He wants us to accept His gift of salvation.

MEMORY VERSE

Don't worry about anything,
but in everything,
through prayer and
petition with thanksgiving,
let your requests be
made known to God.

–Philippians 4:6

ANSWERED AND UNANSWERED PRAYERS

Isn't prayer a pretty wonderful thing? It's the perfect way to praise God, talk with Him, and let Him hear your requests. But sometimes we can be greedy and selfish in our prayers. We want more than what God gives us, and we think our plans are better than His.

Imagine asking your mom to allow you to eat nothing but s'mores for a whole week. That sounds pretty good, doesn't it? She says yes and gives you nothing but s'mores. On Monday, you love them. The rich, milky chocolate tastes so good. You enjoy the way the gooey marshmallow oozes out onto your fingers, and you don't mind the graham cracker crumbs on your shirt. But by Friday, you are so sick of s'mores that you might even eat broccoli! The chocolate tastes too sweet, the marshmallow is too sticky, and your shirt is a crummy mess. In real life, your mom would probably say no to a s'more diet because she knows it's not the best for you.

In much the same way, God knows what's best for us. He expects us to trust Him with not only our prayers but also with the answers. Some prayerful requests may receive a "Yes!" Others will get a "Sorry, no." And some might receive a "Not right now."

When your prayer is not answered the way you hoped, don't get upset and say, "God! Why aren't You giving me what I want?" Instead, remember that God loves you so much and knows which requests fit with His plan for you. No matter how your prayer is answered, go back to God and thank Him for listening and for taking care of you. End your prayer this way: "God, You know what I want, but please give me what I need."

Ask your kids!

LET'S TALK

What do you ask for the most in your prayers?

Has God always given you what you asked for?

Ask your parents!

FAMILY FUN

CRAFTY CREATION

Get together and make a family prayer request book. This can be a simple notebook with a decorated cover or a fancy book you make yourself. Family members should use the book to write down their needs. Check the book every day, and pray for each other's needs. Do your prayers line up with what you know is right?

WEEKLY CHALLENGE

God, give them strength

It is good to pray for your own needs as well as those in your family. But other people need prayer too.

Your challenge this week is to notice when people need something and then pray for them. These can be people you know or strangers. Do you see someone who looks tired? Say a silent prayer, and ask God to give him rest. Do you have a friend who is afraid of something? Ask God to take away her fear. At the end of the week, get together as a family and make a list of all the people you prayed for. End by praying together for everyone on the list.

Read what happened when the Israelites prayed for a king in 1 Samuel 8–10.

CHECKPOINT!

We are learning how to pray for ourselves and for others.

MEMORY VERSE

Let us lay aside every
weight and the sin that
so easily ensnares us.
Let us run with
endurance the race that
lies before us.

—Hebrews 12:1

COACH GOD

"What's the matter, Ty?" his dad asked. "You don't look very happy."

Ty wasn't happy. In fact, he would do just about anything to get out of his Little League game. "We're playing the Comets today," he said, "and they always win."

"Always?" his dad asked.

Ty barely whispered, "Always. They've got the best hitter in the league and a great coach."

"And your team has the best captain–you!" said his dad. "It's your job to encourage your teammates."

Ty hadn't thought about that. Being his team's captain was important. As captain, he needed to encourage his team to stand up to the Comets and convince his fellow players they could win.

"Remember David and Goliath?" said Dad.

Ty did remember. David was the kid in the Bible who stood up to an evil, nine-foot-tall soldier and defeated him with his slingshot. Nobody thought David could do it. But he did because God helped him. "I'll do my best to give the team confidence," Ty said. "And I'll put my faith in God. He always wins."

Take a look at this week's memory verse, Hebrews 12:1. What has you "ensnared"? Are you nervous about the big game like Ty was? Are you facing a big bully like David did? No matter what trouble you're up against, God promises to give you all the strength you need to fight against it. You don't have to be afraid to step up to your enemies and your fears, because God is on your side all the time. He's the perfect Coach.

God is always prepared to call the next play, and you can be sure it's the right one. Putting your trust in God gives you hope. You might not always win the game, but with God as your leader, you will learn to fight fair and give it your best.

Ask your kids!

LET'S TALK

If you were Ty, how would you encourage your team?

When you were a kid, did you play sports? Did you win?

Ask your parents!

FAMILY FUN

BIRDBRAIN IDEA

Draw a picture of that nine-foot-tall soldier, Goliath. Put the picture faceup on the floor. Stand several feet away and take turns tossing small stones or pennies, trying to get them to land on Goliath's head. Give yourself two points when you do. Which player will be first to reach ten points?

WEEKLY CHALLENGE

Talk about this week's memory verse, Hebrews 12:1. We all have some sort of trouble that gets in our way. It might be a hard subject in school, a bad habit, or maybe a difficult person. Talk about how trusting God might help you to deal with and overcome your trouble. Remember: It isn't as important to God that you win as it is for you to put your faith and trust in Him and try your best.

Read more about David in your Bible in 1 Samuel 16–17.

CHECKPOINT!

We learned to face our challenges and trust God to help us.

MEMORY VERSE

Now if any of you lacks wisdom, he should ask God, who gives to all generously and without criticizing, and it will be given to him.

–James 1:5

A WORD TO THE WISE

Do you know the difference between being smart and being wise? A person can become smart by studying hard and learning. You might be smart because you know a lot about many things. But there is a big difference between knowing things and putting them to good use. A wise person can do that.

Think about this. You want to be a pilot, so you read books and watch videos about what a pilot does. You learn about what's in the cockpit, you can name all the controls, and you know what they do. You study really hard and, in time, you become an expert on how to be a pilot. You are smart about what they do. But would it be wise for you to think that you could hop into the cockpit of a 747 and fly the plane? No. Becoming a pilot is more than just learning from books. It requires training. There is a difference between knowing a lot about something and actually doing it.

Learning about the Bible is no different. Some people read the Bible from cover to cover and know a lot about what's in there, but they still don't believe in God. Those "scholars" are smart about knowing what the Bible says but not wise about putting it to use.

The Bible is filled with wisdom. You will find God's wisdom on every single page. That's why it's so important to read your Bible every day and study its words. Let those words sink in and change the ways you feel and act. Then use what you learn to help others so they will know God more. That's real wisdom!

Wisdom is a gift from God. Learning from ordinary books is important, but God cares more about us learning from His book, the Bible, and letting its words give us real wisdom that we can use to do good things.

So, how about it? When it comes to reading the Bible, are you smart, or are you wise?

Who is the wisest person you know?

Ask your kids!

Do you think you're wise?

Ask your parents!

FAMILY FUN

LOOK FOR IT

Did you know that there's a Bible verse about wisdom that talks about dogs and pigs? Let's find it:

- Go to the first book in the New Testament.
- Then find the first chapter in that book that rhymes with *eleven*.
- Next find the verse that is the same number as three sets of twins.
- Read the verse aloud. What do you think it means?

Dogs and pigs?

I've never met a pig!

WEEKLY CHALLENGE

Some of God's wisdom is disguised as a little story or riddle. This is one way that God works to make you wise. The little stories cause you to think really hard, and thinking gives you what? You guessed it—wisdom! Or maybe you said, "a headache."

Read Proverbs 6:6-11 in your Bible. Can you guess what it means? Now think about this one: Proverbs 30:32-33.

Your challenge is to come up with your own little story that teaches something wise. You can work alone or with a partner. Then get together and share your stories.

Read about how Solomon asked God for wisdom in 1 Kings 2:1-4, 10-12; 3:1-15

✔ CHECKPOINT!
We learned that the Bible helps make us wise.

MEMORY VERSE

I have written these things to you who believe in the name of the Son of God, so that you may know that you have eternal life.

—1 John 5:13

WELL DONE!

Rules are important because they keep life running smoothly. What if there were no rules for playing basketball? Players would run every which way on the court, tossing balls and making baskets. No one would win if there were no rules. What if there were no rules for cars, trains, or planes? Crashes would happen everywhere. If there were no rules at the zoo, people would climb in with the animals and try to pet them—well, maybe not wise people—but you get the idea: the world needs rules.

What are the rules at your house? Do you always follow them? What happens if you don't? Your mom makes rules because she loves you. She wants to teach you to be safe and responsible. Your parents know that following the rules will help you to grow up to be a better adult, one who loves God and is excited about the future He has for you.

God is the same kind of parent. He makes rules because He loves you and wants to teach you right from wrong. His rules are there to care for you and help you enjoy the blessings He has planned for you—blessings like the joy that comes from knowing Him, forgiveness when you mess up, and, as this week's memory verse reminds us, the future promise of living in heaven with Him someday. Those are great reasons to obey the rules.

As you read your Bible, pay close attention to God's rules about right and wrong. Getting His Word into your heart and keeping it there is important. When you know what God expects of you, then it will be easier for you to follow His rules and obey Him.

Think about all the ways that God has blessed you with family, friends, good food, and warm clothes. Pray and ask God to help you obey the rules. Then do your best to behave in the ways that please Him.

Which of our rules is the easiest to follow? Which is the hardest?

When you were a kid, did you ever break a rule? Did you get in trouble?

Ask your kids!

Ask your parents!

FAMILY FUN
ACT IT OUT

Act out these situations with a partner.
- You find a ten-dollar bill on the sidewalk. What would you do?
- Mom says you can't have a snack before dinner, but she isn't watching, and it would be so easy to grab a cookie. What would you do?
- You see a friend steal something, and he says, "Don't you tell!" What would you do?
- You're at a friend's house, and he wants to watch a show that your parents don't allow you to watch. What would you do?

WEEKLY CHALLENGE

Can you imagine life without instructions? Nothing would work properly. People would be running around like crazy, not knowing which way to go.

Think of a certain object in your house and then give instructions to another family member for how to find it. Use things like, "Take two steps to the left," "Turn around," "Turn right," and so on. When the family member follows your instructions and finds the object, reward him or her with a hug.

Talk about why it is important to follow God's instructions and rules in the Bible. How can those rules help you and actually bring you blessings?

Read a story about how a man named Naaman had to obey instructions in 2 Kings 5.

CHECKPOINT!

We know that God makes rules because He loves us and wants us to live with Him in heaven someday.

MEMORY VERSE

For God has not given us
a spirit of fearfulness,
but one of power, love,
and sound judgment.

—2 Timothy 1:7

RIGHT HERE, RIGHT NOW

What are you doing right now? You are reading this, or someone is reading it to you. That might not seem like a big deal, but it is because God put you right here right now as part of His plan. God has you right where He wants you. Right here right now you might be learning something important about Him, something that you will use in some way to serve Him.

This week's memory verse, 2 Timothy 1:7, reminds us that in whatever situation God puts us, He empowers us through His love. When we trust Him, we can believe that God will help us make the right decisions and act on them instead of backing away in fear.

Sylvie was at a sleepover with some friends when they started doing things that Sylvie's parents did not approve of. One of the girls went on the computer and logged into a chat room. Then some of the girls pretended to be much older, and they started chatting with people online.

Sylvie got a sick feeling in her stomach. She was scared. She didn't know what to do because all the girls, even some Sylvie knew were Christians, went along with what was happening.

Sylvie said a prayer. "God, please help me with this." Then she decided to put her faith in Him and do what she knew was right. Instead of sitting there afraid, Sylvie said, "Guys, I don't think we should be doing this." And then one of her Christian friends agreed. And then another. The girls ended up sharing their faith with the one who first got on the computer, and they led her into a relationship with Jesus. Isn't it wonderful that Sylvie spoke up?

Sylvie was in the right place at the right time. And so are you! You can't know the plans God has for you, but you must trust Him and let Him do the rest. Always be brave and do what is right. Trust God to use you. He has you right where He wants you all the time.

Have you ever told a friend about God?

Ask your kids!

Have you ever been afraid to admit that you love God?

Ask your parents!

FAMILY FUN

CRAFTY CREATION

Faith has the power to crush fear. Faith is bigger and more powerful than a monster truck or any make-believe superhero. This week, draw a picture of your super family wearing superhero costumes. You can even come up with hero names! Put the picture in your room to remind you that faith in God gives you the power to squash fear whenever it gets in your way.

WEEKLY CHALLENGE

Get together as a family and discuss why it is important to share your faith with others and ways that you can do it. Then promise to talk about God with at least one friend this week. God will put you in just the right place at the right time. Maybe you know someone who is struggling with a problem. Tell your friend that God can help. Or maybe you know someone who is lonely. You might tell them that God loves them. Never be afraid to share your love of God. Trust Him to make you brave.

Look in your Bible to read about Esther, a courageous woman whom God put in the right place at the right time in Esther 4:1–5:14; 7:1–10.

CHECKPOINT!

We learned that we can be brave because God has us right where He wants us.

MEMORY VERSE

In the beginning was the Word, and the Word was with God, and the Word was God.

—John 1:1

JESUS!

Name everyone who is there in the room with you.

Did you remember to include God? What about Jesus? God is there, and Jesus is there too because He is part of the Trinity. That means Jesus was there when the heavens and the earth were created. And it means He will be here always and forever.

In Old Testament times, God's people, the Jews, had not heard of Jesus. That's because it wasn't time yet for God to reveal the Jesus part of His plan— and a wonderful part it was! God's people couldn't help themselves from sinning, and as long as they misbehaved, there was no way they could get into heaven. God does not allow sin there. So God made a way for people to get to heaven. He planned to send Jesus to earth to save the people from sin.

God began giving people hints that Jesus was coming. (God often does that. He gives us bits of information about the future. You will find those in the Bible too.) God spoke to men and women called prophets. He gave them some information about Jesus so they would know to expect Him. God wanted them to look forward to it just as much as you look forward to Christmas and opening your presents.

The prophet Isaiah was someone to whom God often spoke about Jesus. God told Isaiah hints about who Jesus' mother would be, where Jesus would be born, and that Jesus would give up His own life to save His people from sin. Isaiah shared this information with the people.

Do you think the people believed Isaiah? Some did. Some did not. People are still the same today—some believe in Jesus, and some do not.

Do you believe? I hope so, because along with the Bible, Jesus is your very best friend. You can trust Him with everything. And, oh, how He loves you!

What do you know about Jesus?

Ask your kids!

Do you believe in Jesus? Did you always?

Ask your parents!

FAMILY FUN
LOOK FOR IT

Jesus is sometimes called the Prince of _____.
Fill in the blank by using these clues:

• Go to Isaiah's book in the Old Testament.
• Find the correct chapter by adding the number 1 to the
  number of wings you'd count on four birds.
• Then read the verse whose number rhymes with
  the word *chicks*.

The prince of Wales, maybe?

No, that's not it.

WEEKLY CHALLENGE

Have fun this week making up funny (but kind) predictions about your family members. You might say things like, "This week I predict that Dad will become a famous rock star," or "This week I predict that Mom will allow us to eat a dozen cookies every night."

Talk about the differences between made-up predictions and the real prophecies in the Bible. God revealed Himself through His prophets. To prove it was Him speaking, He sometimes gave them prophecies— a peek at the future. Those prophecies and everything else in the Bible are true, unlike your predictions about eating cookies!

Also, talk about this week's memory verse. "The Word" is another name for Jesus. The Word was with God in the beginning.

Read more Old Testament hints about Jesus in Isaiah 7:1-14; 9:1-7; 11:1-5; and Micah 5:2.

✓ CHECKPOINT!

We believe that God sent His Son, Jesus, to save people from sin.

MEMORY VERSE

"Do not say, 'I am only a youth,' for you will go to everyone I send you to and speak whatever I tell you."

−Jeremiah 1:7

GOD'S KIDS

When something seems too hard, you might try to get out of it by saying, "But I'm just a kid!" Usually, that doesn't work because a grown-up will help you. Parents and teachers know that doing hard things is one way you learn and grow. Plus, sometimes God has big plans for us that aren't always easy.

What if that kid, David, the one who killed the horrible giant Goliath, had said, "I'm just a kid," and walked away? The Israelites might have lost the battle, and history would have been changed forever. But God did not let that happen. He gave a kid the power to do something great. God loves kids, and He uses them just as much as grown-ups to carry out His plans.

The Bible tells the story of a kid named Jeremiah whom God chose to be a prophet. When God called on him, Jeremiah said, "But I'm just a kid!"

God answered, "Do not say, 'I am only a kid,' for you will go to everyone I send you to and speak whatever I tell you. Do not be afraid of anyone, for I will be with you." Then God began telling Jeremiah stuff, things about the future that He wanted Jeremiah to tell the people. "Now stand up and get going," God said. "Tell the people what I told you, and do not let them make you afraid!"

What if God called on you? Would you say, "But I'm just a kid"? Would you do what God asked, or would you run away?

God will never ask you to do anything foolish that causes you or others harm. But God might ask you to do something hard.

You are not just a kid; you are God's kid! When you face a hard task doing something that you know is right, don't run away or be afraid. Doing the right thing is always a part of God's plan for you. Stand up and get going. If someone or something gets in your way, you can always call on God for help. He is the One who gives you power to do everything–even when it's hard.

Ask your kids!

Can you name one really hard thing you've learned to do?

What is something hard you did when you were a kid?

Ask your parents!

FAMILY FUN

BIRDBRAIN IDEA

Kids can help God _____ ____ _____.
Decode this message to finish the sentence. Replace each letter with the letter that follows it in the alphabet. Hint: Z=A

B G Z M F D   S G D   V N Q K C

Parlez-vous Français?

Oui -

Wee!

The challenge this week is for each family member to learn something new, something that is not very easy. In the first chapter of this book, you learned to memorize the books of the Bible. This week, you might challenge yourself to learn five new Scripture verses or write ten letters to elderly people at your church. Or maybe you can try to make a new recipe or learn to say hello in ten languages. Don't be afraid to try. Ask for help.

At the end of the week, get together with your family and talk about what you have learned. Have you stayed with the task? Did you ask God to help you?

God called Jeremiah to do something big. Read about it in Jeremiah 1.

✔ CHECKPOINT!

We discovered that God gives us power to do difficult things, even when we're young.

MEMORY VERSE

For the wages of sin
is death, but the gift
of God is eternal life
in Christ Jesus
our Lord.

–Romans 6:23

DANCING BONES

This week's memory verse is about God's gift of eternal life. Do you know what *eternal life* means? Maybe you are like Dylan. He wasn't sure until his youth pastor told this story about the prophet Ezekiel's dream.

Everywhere Ezekiel looked, he saw dead, dry bones lying on the ground. God said to Ezekiel, "Do you think these bones can come to life?"

"Only You know," Ezekiel answered.

Then God told Ezekiel to tell those bones: "Dry bones, hear the word of the Lord! The Lord says, 'I will cause breath to enter you, and you will live. I will put tendons on you, make flesh grow on you, and cover you with skin. You will come to life. Then you will know that I am God.'"

When Ezekiel spoke God's words, those dead, dry bones rattled. They shimmied. They shook. They came together, bone to bone. Then God covered the skeletons with flesh and skin. He blew breath into those lifeless bodies, and they lived again! They became a mighty army standing before Ezekiel.

Wow! Dylan thought it was the coolest Bible story he had ever heard. But Pastor Tom wasn't finished yet. Pastor said, "There is an important message in Ezekiel's story, a message about Jesus. If someone dies without knowing Jesus, they become nothing but a pile of dead, dry bones, and they stay like that forever. But if a person dies believing in Jesus, then their souls go to heaven forever."

Dylan got it! Believing in Jesus is the only way to get to heaven, and heaven is where we live forever, for always, for eternity with God.

But what about our bodies? Well, the Bible says that someday in the future—we don't know when—God will raise the dead bodies of believers and make them new again, like the bones in Ezekiel's dream. Then we all will have new, strong healthy bodies, forever.

Isn't Jesus a wonderful gift? Because of Him, we will never die; we have eternal life. How do we know? Because God says so. It is His promise.

LET'S TALK

If God gave you a strange dream, like Ezekiel's, and told you to share it, would you? Why?

Ask your kids!

What do you think it is like to live forever in heaven?

Ask your parents!

FAMILY FUN

ACT IT OUT

Those dry bones began to rattle. They shimmied. They shook. They came together, bone to bone! Get the whole family together and make up a dance about those dry bones standing up and putting themselves together again. Then have fun and dance . . . dance . . . dance!

Jesus is the One who gives us hope of living forever. Without Him, all of us would die and not go to heaven. That's because humans sin, and there is no place for sin in heaven. God didn't want that to happen to us, so He sent Jesus to take our sin away.

Discuss what it means to have hope in Jesus. This week, each family member should come up with an idea for one small object they can carry in their pocket as a reminder of their hope in Him. Get together and talk about what you chose and why.

Read the story of Ezekiel and the dry bones in Ezekiel 37.

✔ CHECKPOINT!
We know that if we believe in Jesus, we will live with Him forever.

MEMORY VERSE

Great is the LORD and most worthy of praise; his greatness no one can fathom.

–Psalm 145:3

NIV

GREAT IS OUR GOD

Do you enjoy going to concerts to hear your favorite singers? Or maybe you love sporting events like football or auto racing. Isn't it exciting being with others and joining in with all the shouting, cheering, and clapping? Singers and sports stars find it exciting too. Everyone enjoys a little praise.

But there is Someone who deserves praise more than anyone or anything else. God! He is greater than your most favorite singer, sports star, or anyone. He is the one and only God. No one is as great as He.

Psalm 145:3 reminds us to praise God for His greatness, and one way we do that is through worship—honoring God by telling Him how wonderful we know He is and thanking Him for His blessings. We worship Him because He blesses us with love, happiness, comfort, wisdom, strength, patience, protection, forgiveness, hope, and so much more. We don't deserve any of those things. They are God's gifts to us.

If I asked you, "What is God's greatest gift?" what would you say? If your answer is Jesus, then you're right! Humans messed up so badly that God could never allow them to bring their messes into heaven. So, because God loves us, He sent His only Son down to earth as part of His plan to save the world. We worship God because He loves us so much that He wants us with Him forever, and not only with Him but also free of that mess called sin.

And God's great gift is only one reason He deserves our praise. Kings, queens, presidents, Oscar winners, Super-Bowl stars—no one is more worthy than God. Worship Him by living in a way that pleases Him. Worship Him by singing and praying and reading the Bible.

Take a minute right now to worship God. Thank Him for being your One and Only. Tell Him how much you love Him.

Ask your kids!

If you could be a famous person, who would you be?

Who was your favorite celebrity when you were a kid?

Ask your parents!

FAMILY FUN

CRAFTY CREATION

Make a worship banner. Cut out four large paper triangles. Write one word on each: *We. Worship. God. Together.* Decorate the triangles and then tape them horizontally onto a long piece of string or ribbon. Hang up your banner for everyone to see.

WEEKLY CHALLENGE

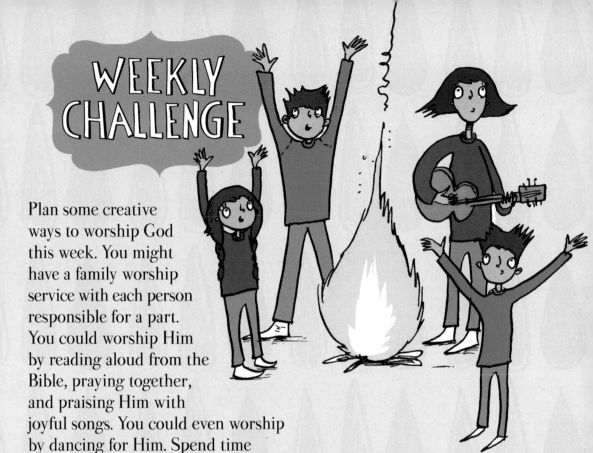

Plan some creative ways to worship God this week. You might have a family worship service with each person responsible for a part. You could worship Him by reading aloud from the Bible, praying together, and praising Him with joyful songs. You could even worship by dancing for Him. Spend time together outdoors noticing some of His creations. Call out the names of the things you see. Could any human create them? Talk about how great God is. Then give Him some praise for all His good gifts.

Go to Daniel 3 in your Bible and read about three men who refused to worship anyone or anything other than God!

CHECKPOINT!

We focused on praising God more each day.

MEMORY VERSE

"Stop your fighting—
and know that I am
God, exalted among the
nations, exalted on
the earth."

–Psalm 46:10

FIGHT THE GOOD FIGHT

"Jeremy and Caden, stop fighting!"

Their mom must have said that to the brothers a dozen times. Jeremy and Caden loved each other, but they seemed to fight everyday. One of the brothers always seemed to want what the other had.

Have you ever argued with someone in your family? Or maybe a teammate? People have been arguing and fighting since all the way back in Bible times. In the book of Genesis, we learn that God promised His people, the Jews, their own homeland. But after He gave it to them, keeping it theirs was not easy. Other nations wanted that land for their own. Armies came and fought with the Jews to take their land. And that fighting continues to this day.

God wants us to be careful that what we fight for lines up with what He wants and not what we want. Bad fighting is usually the result of someone's selfishness and pride, like wanting to take something that belongs to someone else. Good fighting is when we stand up for what we know God wants. Some of the things worth fighting for are protecting our families, for example a neighborhood watch committee. Another good fight is defending innocent people, like standing up to help someone who is being bullied. Another good reason to fight is standing up for freedom, the right to have your own opinions about God and everything else.

Jeremy and Caden's mom taught them to solve their disagreements in other ways: sharing with each other, talking out their problems, and asking God for a solution. God likes it when people work out their difficulties that way. He loves peace. It is one of His gifts, something He promises us when we put our faith in Him and obey His rules.

The Bible teaches you God's rules, and when you know them, obey them, and trust God, He will teach you to always fight fair and stand up for what's right.

LET'S TALK

Other than fighting, what are some ways of standing up for what you believe?

Ask your kids!

Have you stood up for something you believe in?

Ask your parents!

FAMILY FUN

BIRDBRAIN IDEA

The Bible tells us that God saved a man named Daniel who stood up for his faith, fought for God, and was thrown into a den of hungry lions. Choose one room in your house to be a lions' den. One person, Daniel, goes into that room. The other people, lions, each go to a different room in the house. The lions roar, one at a time, and Daniel must guess in which rooms they are.

WEEKLY CHALLENGE

FOR YOU

When you stand up for God, like Daniel in the Bible did, God promises to help you. When you fight for what is right, God is always on your side.

This week, make a plan for your family to stand up for a cause you believe in. Do you want to fight hunger? Contribute to a food bank. Do you want to fight loneliness? Visit residents in a nursing home and bring them a little gift. What other ways can you think of to stand up and fight for what's right?

In Daniel 6, read about what happened to Daniel when he stood up for God and refused to bow down to a king.

✓ CHECKPOINT!

We will stand firm, fight the good fight, and obey God.

MEMORY VERSE

God proves His own love for us in that while we were still sinners, Christ died for us!

–Romans 5:8

MESS-UPS AND MERCY

Do you know what the word *mercy* means? It means not getting the punishment you deserve.

Every kid on earth messes up sometimes. Let's say you mess up the first time and your parents let you off with a warning. That's mercy. You did not get punished. But if your parents tell you a bunch of times not to do something and you keep on doing it, you probably won't get any mercy from them. You will receive the punishment that's coming to you.

Chris's parents gave him a cell phone. Chris was only supposed to use his phone to stay in touch with his parents or for emergencies. But one day he used it to call a friend, and Chris's parents found out.

"It was an emergency," Chris explained. "I needed to make afterschool plans."

Instead of punishing Chris, his parents explained that an emergency was not calling a friend to make plans. They did not punish Chris. They showed mercy and gave him another chance.

God has mercy on us too. When we sin, He gives us the opportunity to try again. The Bible includes many stories of second chances. Do you remember the one about Jonah and the big fish? Jonah messed up and was swallowed by the fish because he disobeyed God. But, after three days in the fish's belly, God made the fish spit Jonah out. He gave Jonah another chance to obey.

The memory verse this week reminds us that all are sinners and deserving of punishment, but God sent Jesus to save us. Jesus is God's mercy and forgiveness. Jesus loves us so much that He took all of the punishment that we deserve, and it cost Him His life. Jesus died being punished for all of the bad stuff we do. It was God's way of washing us clean of sin so we are ready for heaven someday. God is so merciful to us that He gave up His only Son. Wow, that's love!

What do you think it was like for Jonah sitting inside the belly of that fish?

Ask your kids!

Ask your parents!

Was there a time when you disobeyed and someone showed you mercy?

FAMILY FUN

CRAFTY CREATION

Draw a picture of other things that you think might have been in the fish's belly with Jonah. Who knows what else that big fish swallowed! Have fun thinking about and drawing what might be inside, and don't be afraid to be silly. Now say a little prayer and thank God for second chances.

Assign a chore to each family member for each day this week. These can be things like setting the table or taking out the trash. Use blank paper to make a set of cards, as many cards as there are family members. Write *Do it* on all but one card and *Mercy* on the last. Every day this week, spread the cards facedown. Have each family member choose one. The person who gets the Mercy card gets out of doing his or her chore that day.

Talk about some of the ways that God shows us mercy. How can we be merciful to others?

Read Jonah's story in Jonah 1–4.

CHECKPOINT!

We learned that God is forgiving and merciful.

125

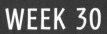

MEMORY VERSE

For nothing will be impossible with God.

–Luke 1:37

JESUS IS COMING!

Everything you've learned about the Bible so far has led to this: God sending His Son, Jesus, to save the world.

God could have planned a big announcement: *Jesus is coming! Jesus is coming!* But instead, He sent an angel to tell a humble young woman named Mary that He chose her to be Jesus' mom. Imagine an angel popping up from nowhere right in front of you. Would you be afraid? Mary was.

Looking from the outside, she was no one special. Mary was not a queen, or a princess, or anyone famous. She was just an ordinary young woman engaged to marry Joseph, an ordinary young man, but God saw that she had a servant's heart. It shouldn't surprise you that God chose Mary. You already know that He uses ordinary people to do extraordinary things. This time, God planned for an ordinary woman to give birth to His one and only Son.

"Nothing is impossible for God," the angel told Mary. And it's true—God can do absolutely anything. If He decides to use you in some way, He will find a way to make it possible.

Think about some Bible stories you know. God made it possible for Noah to build a gigantic ark big enough to hold all those animals. God gave young David the bravery and strength to strike down the giant Goliath. God sealed shut the lions' mouths so they couldn't eat poor Daniel. And now God was setting another of His great plans into action, the greatest one of all. He was sending us Jesus, and God chose an ordinary woman, much like your mom, aunt, or sister, to bring Him into the world.

You see, no one is ordinary to God. He makes each of us special, including you. If God calls on you to do something that seems impossible, He wants you to do what Mary did and say, "I will do whatever You want, God." When you say yes to Him, He will make a way. When you put your trust in God, everything becomes possible.

Can you name five things God can do that a person can't do?

Ask your kids!

Has God ever helped you do something that you thought was impossible?

Ask your parents!

FAMILY FUN

LOOK FOR IT

Replace what is inside the ( ) with the correct word.

The story of (the Son of God) is told in the (opposite of *last*) (10 − 8 + 2 =) (things you read) in the (opposite of *old*) Testament. Each one is named for a (opposite of *woman*). What are their names?

Rover? Spot? Fido? Rocky?

I don't think so!

WEEKLY CHALLENGE

Humility means not thinking that you are better than anyone else. Mary's story is about humility. She was a humble young woman who understood that anything great she accomplished came from God.

Maybe you have heard an athlete or actor accept an award and say, "All the glory goes to God." That person is showing humility. He or she understands that God makes it possible for us to do great things.

Discuss ways that people show humility (treating others equally, politeness, forgiveness, kindness, and more). Ask God to help you be humble this week. At the end of the week, talk about what you have learned.

Read more of Mary's story in Luke 1:26–56 and Matthew 1:18–24.

CHECKPOINT!

We know that all things are possible with God.

MEMORY VERSE

Today a Savior, who is Messiah the Lord, was born for you in the city of David.

—Luke 2:11

GOD'S GIFT TO THE WORLD

As soon as a baby is born or adopted, parents send a text or call people and say, "Our child is here!" It's how they share the good news.

When our heavenly Father shared the news that His Son was born, there were no cell phones. But who needs a phone when you have angels! God sent angels to shepherds nearby, and the angels said, "Today a Savior, who is Messiah the Lord, was born for you in the city of David." The shepherds shared the good news with others, and then those people shared the news, and, before long, a whole bunch of people knew that a special baby had been born in Bethlehem, the City of David. That baby was the One God promised –the Savior, the Messiah.

Are you confused about what those words *Savior* and *Messiah* mean? Dawn was, so she asked the youth pastor at her church.

"A savior is someone who saves you from something," said Pastor Nate. "Like when a firefighter saves someone from a burning building. But Jesus is the most excellent Savior because He saves us from sin. No one else can do that. And Messiah means the One whom God chose. In the Old Testament, God used the word *Messiah* when He spoke to the prophets about Jesus."

Dawn learned that there are many different names for Jesus: Shepherd, Messiah, Savior, Lord, and others. But on the day Jesus was born, His Father chose the names Savior and Messiah to announce His birth. You might think of it like those birth announcement cards that parents send. The card has the baby's complete name and other information like the time and sometimes the place where the baby was born. The angels gave that same information to the shepherds: "Today a Savior, who is Messiah the Lord, was born for you in the city of David."

Did you notice that God's birth announcement included the words *born for you*? God sent Jesus as the Savior for all of us. Jesus is God's gift to the world.

Ask your kids!

Of all the gifts you have ever received, which one did you like best?

How did you share the good news when you got me?

Ask your parents!

FAMILY FUN

CRAFTY CREATION

Create a pretty card to announce Jesus' birth. Include His name on the card, the place where He was born, and when. If you find the *when* part tricky, think about the one day each year when we celebrate Jesus' birthday. Hint: It comes at the end of December. Think about saving your cards and sending them as Christmas cards this year.

When Jesus grew up, He said, "My sheep hear My voice, I know them, and they follow Me" (John 10:27). What do you think Jesus meant? This week's challenge is to play the Shepherd Game. Choose a different leader (shepherd) each day to do things like lead your family's dinnertime conversation or lead them in prayer. Shepherds should also lead their "sheep" in doing one little fun activity of their choosing—something simple like reading a story together or playing charades.

Were you a good leader? Did your "sheep" do a good job following you?

Now you know where to find the story about Jesus' birth. It's in Luke 2:1-20.

✔ CHECKPOINT!

We know that God sent Jesus to be our Shepherd and our Savior.

☐

MEMORY VERSE

The heavens declare the glory of God, and the sky proclaims the work of His hands.

–Psalm 19:1

LOOK UP

On that ordinary night when Jesus was born, God used His sky in very extraordinary ways. He opened it up so angels could come down to the shepherds in a brilliant, white light. Then God hung a bright, dazzling star in the sky over Bethlehem to mark the place where Jesus was. And far away from Bethlehem, some of the wisest men on earth noticed that star. The wise men followed it for months knowing that it would lead them to Jesus, the Messiah whom God had promised. In the time when Jesus was born, a lot of people were looking up at the sky.

Our memory verse this week, Psalm 19:1, reminds us to look up at the sky, too, and to think about God. He hung the moon and the sun up there. He scattered the stars. God even knows the name of each one. How grand is that? Could you count and name all those stars?

Humans know a lot about the earth, but God's sky is still a mystery. We have walked on the moon. We know a little about Mars from a robot we sent up there to take a closer look. Astronauts live in the International Space Station. But the sky is a massive, ginormous place, and we only know a sliver of what's up there. God knows the rest.

God wants us to look up and see His greatness in the sky. When we look up and see what God has done, we remember that although He often works quietly, using ordinary people to accomplish His plans, our God is extraordinary. He does extraordinary things, like long ago when He hung a bright star in the sky—a star that led to our Shepherd, Jesus, the One whom God sent to save the world.

What do you think is in the sky beyond the moon and stars?

Ask your kids!

When you were a kid, did you ever want to be an astronaut?

Ask your parents!

FAMILY FUN

BIRDBRAIN IDEA

The sky is amazing both night and day. Spend some time looking at the sky. (Don't look directly at the sun, though!) Now make a list of God's creations that you see up there. Look for ordinary things (like the color blue) along with the extraordinary (an oddly shaped cloud). Who can make the longest list? Hint: Some of God's creations are always up in the sky, and others just fly by.

CAMEL

Have fun acting out the wise men's trip. Can you find a very long path through, around, and into your house? Maybe you can pretend your dog is a camel (just don't ride him!). Should you stop along the way and ask for directions?

Now, talk about it. What do you imagine it was like for the wise men to see such an incredible star? What do you think it looked like? Do you think their long journey was fun? Or way too tiring?

The wise men lived long ago. What ways does God use His sky to get our attention today?

Go to Matthew 2:1–21 to read more about the wise men's journey to find Jesus.

CHECKPOINT!

We learned that we have an extraordinary God.

MEMORY VERSE

And a voice came from heaven: You are My beloved Son; I take delight in You!

–Mark 1:11

HOW DELIGHTFUL

Alex was happy to have a day off from school, but he also felt a little bit nervous. It was parent-teacher conference day, the first of the school year. Alex liked his teacher, and he thought he was doing okay. But he wasn't sure. Math was a challenge for Alex, but he tried really hard and did his best. Alex hoped that when his mom and dad got home from the conference, they would have good news. He waited, looking at the clock. *I wonder what they're talking about,* he said to himself. *Mom and Dad have been gone a long time.*

When he heard his parents' car come into the garage, Alex's stomach did a flip-flop. When they opened the door, he smelled pizza. That was a good sign. He couldn't wait to find out, so while his mom carried the pizza into the kitchen, Alex blurted out, "So, what did Mrs. Bruno say?"

Dad smiled and winked at Alex. "She says you're a delight to have in her class."

And Mom called from the kitchen, "We think you're delightful too."

Parents are proud of their children, and God is no different. The Bible tells us that God was proud of His Son when He got baptized in the Jordan River. Jesus was immersed and then came up out of the water. When He did, God opened up the sky, and Jesus saw God's Spirit coming down from heaven like a dove. God's voice said to Jesus, "You are My beloved Son; I take delight in You!"

God is delighted in Jesus, but He is also delighted when any of His children please Him. The Bible tells us that God delights in every detail of our lives (Psalm 37:23 NLT). He was delighted when Alex got a good report from his teacher, and God is delighted when you do well.

Try hard and do your best to please God. Then, when you meet Him in heaven someday, you might hear His voice say, "My beloved child, I'm delighted with *you*."

How do you think you're doing in school?

Ask your kids!

Do you think I'm delightful?

Ask your parents!

FAMILY FUN
LOOK FOR IT

In another place in the Bible God calls Jesus His beloved Son, and He gives us an instruction:
"This is My beloved Son. I take delight in Him. _____!"

Are you listening?

Use the clues below to discover what Scripture to read to fill in the blank above.
- One of the first two books of the New Testament. Not Mark, but _____. (This is your book.)
- Sophia is 16. She will be ___ next year. (This is your chapter.)
- One, two, three, ___, ___, ___, seven, eight. (Read these verses.)

Alex and his family celebrated his good news with a pizza. What are some other ways that they might have celebrated?

People have many occasions to celebrate. Baptism is one of them. Christians celebrate when someone is baptized because baptism connects that person with Jesus. It says to the world, "I belong to Him! Jesus died so I can be forgiven for my sins, and I will live with Him in heaven someday."

This week, celebrate your belief in Jesus by having an I Love Jesus day. Do something fun together as a family. Take time to talk about Jesus and the reasons you love Him.

Read about Jesus' baptism in Matthew 3:1-6; 13-17; Mark 1:9-11; and Luke 3:21-22.

✔ CHECKPOINT!

We learned that God takes delight in the good things we do.

MEMORY VERSE

Surely goodness and mercy shall follow me all the days of my life: and I will dwell in the house of the LORD for ever.

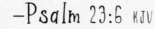

–Psalm 23:6 KJV

WHERE DOES GOD LIVE?

What do you think of when you hear the word *church*? Maybe the word causes you to think of a church building with stained glass windows and a tall steeple on its roof. Or maybe it reminds you of your own church and the friends you have there. The church–all churches–are where people come together to worship God. Even before Jesus was born, there was a church. God's people, the Jews, called it the temple, and that's where they went to honor God.

When Jesus was just a young boy, He went with His parents to the temple. Jesus felt really at home there. He enjoyed listening to the teachers, learning from them, and asking questions. Jesus called the temple His Father's house.

Are you like Jesus when He was your age? Do you like going to church or Sunday school class? Do you feel close to God there?

Bible class and church are where you go to learn about Jesus. You discover that He is good and forgiving. You learn that Jesus loves you so much that He follows what you are doing every day of your life. He guides and helps you.

This week's memory verse, Psalm 23:6, reminds us that church is not the only house that God lives in. He lives in the hearts of His children. His forever home is heaven. The Bible teaches us that Jesus gave His own life so we could be free of sin. When we are forgiven, we get to live in heaven someday. After Jesus died, He came back to life. People saw Him, and they were amazed. But Jesus didn't stay here forever. He said He was going back to His Father's house–heaven–to prepare a place for us there. He promised that someday He would come back to take us there to live with Him.

Jesus says there are many mansions in heaven (John 14:2). The mansions there are the most beautiful houses you could ever imagine. If you believe in Jesus, then there is a forever house in heaven waiting just for you.

What do you think our house in heaven will look like?

Ask your kids!

Is heaven big enough for all those houses?

Ask your parents!

BIRDBRAIN IDEA

The boy Jesus went missing. His parents found Him in a temple in which city? Use the code to find out.

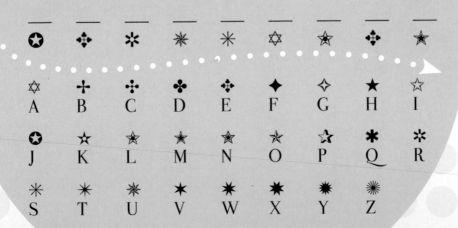

✪	✛	❋	✳	✳	✡	★	✛	★

✡	✚	✜	♣	✛	◆	✧	★	☆
A	B	C	D	E	F	G	H	I

✪	☆	☆	☆	☆	☆	☆	✱	✽
J	K	L	M	N	O	P	Q	R

❋	✳	✳	★	✳	✴	✹	✺	
S	T	U	V	W	X	Y	Z	

WEEKLY CHALLENGE

Have fun as a family making up a rap or a rhyming poem about why church is a good place to be.

Talk about what you like best about your church. Why is it important to listen to and ask questions about what you learn there? Can you think of some ways to be more involved at church?

Read about Jesus in the temple in Luke 2:41-52.

✓ CHECKPOINT!

We learned that Jesus is waiting for us in His home in heaven.

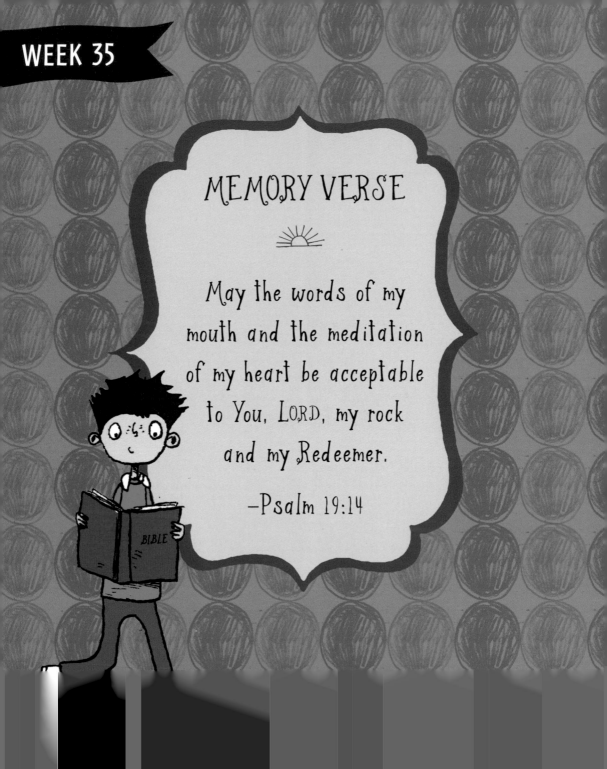

MEMORY VERSE

May the words of my mouth and the meditation of my heart be acceptable to You, LORD, my rock and my Redeemer.

–Psalm 19:14

I DARE YOU

Colton lived in the country where there were hills, valleys, and streams to explore. The country is a lovely place to grow up, but it's also a place where you can get into trouble if you aren't careful. One steep hill was particularly dangerous, and at its foot was a river. Colton and his friends called it Dead Man's Hill.

"Colt, I dare you to ride your bike down Dead Man's Hill," said one of his friends.

No way, Colton thought. He had a reputation for being a daredevil, but Dead Man's Hill made him shiver. Plus, his parents had warned him never to race down it.

"Come on," said another friend. "You can do it."

"Yeah," said a third. "You're not afraid, are you? I dare you."

No way was Colton going to look weak in front of his friends. So, although he knew it was wrong, Colton said, "I'll do it. Watch me!"

Colton flew down the hill on his bike, racing out of control, until *Bam!* He hit a rock and went flying into the river. Colton got hurt, but thankfully he wasn't hurt too badly.

Psalm 19:14 reminds us to think before we act. Our words and thoughts should always be acceptable to God. Do you think God was pleased when Colton disobeyed his parents and raced his bike down Dead Man's Hill or when Colton said, "I'll do it"? Of course not. Accepting that dare was a foolish thing to do, and it ended with Colton getting hurt.

Jesus is the perfect example of what we should do when someone says, "I dare you." Matthew 4 tells about a time the devil took Jesus into the wilderness and dared Him to do things that were wrong. But our Lord knew better. He kept His thoughts focused on God. When the devil said, "I dare you," Jesus answered with a Bible verse: "Do not test the Lord your God" (Matthew 4:7).

The next time you are tempted to do something that you know is wrong, remember what Jesus did. Say no to sin, and say yes to God.

LET'S TALK

What would you do if your friends dared you to do something that you knew was wrong?

Ask your kids!

When you were a kid, did you ever accept a dare?

Ask your parents!

FAMILY FUN

ACT IT OUT

Act out Colton's story and show how he might have handled the dare by keeping his thoughts focused on God. Are there Bible verses you could use to help you resist temptation in the future? Include them when you act out your story.

WEEKLY CHALLENGE

For this week's challenge, you will need an old sheet or another long piece of fabric. Go outside to play a friendly family game of tug-of-war. Split into teams. Mark a midpoint on the grass. Then see which team can pull the other over the midpoint.

Now spend some time talking about temptation. What does it feel like to be pulled toward something you don't want to do? What does it feel like to resist?

Read the story about Jesus standing up to the devil in Matthew 4:1-11; Luke 4:1-13; and Mark 1:12-13.

✓

CHECKPOINT!

We know that God wants us to be wise about our actions and our words.

MEMORY VERSE

"For if you forgive people their wrongdoing, your heavenly Father will forgive you as well."

–Matthew 6:14

I FORGIVE YOU

Destiny was upset to find out that her best friend, Jill, was taking another girl to the amusement park. *Why didn't Jill invite me?* Destiny wondered. *We're best friends!*

A few days later, when Destiny saw Jill, she said, "How come you didn't ask me to come with you?"

Jill got nervous and denied the whole thing. "What? I wasn't at the amusement park," she lied. But after a while she felt bad. She explained that her mom and the other girl's mom were friends, so they planned a family outing together. "It didn't have anything to do with you," Jill said. "I didn't want you to feel left out, so I lied. I'm really sorry."

Destiny's feelings were hurt, but she forgave her friend. But what if Jill lied to Destiny again? Would Destiny forgive her *again*?

Jesus says she should forgive, no matter what. Our memory verse this week is Jesus speaking directly to us. He says, "For if you forgive people their wrongdoing, your heavenly Father will forgive you as well."

If people never forgave each other, everyone would go around angry all the time. That wouldn't be any fun, nor would it be pleasing to God. The Bible says that you should give your hurt and anger to Him and allow Him to do the rest. Leave the punishment up to Him.

Forgiveness comes in all sizes. If someone accidently bumps into you in the hallway at school and says, "I'm sorry," it's easy to forgive and say, "No problem." If your little sister eats the last brownie, the one you wanted, it might be a little harder to say, "I forgive you." Still, you would. Big things like a friend's betrayal seem almost unforgivable. But Jesus says that you must.

When you forgive people, you are not saying that what they did was right. You are showing that God is bigger than your anger and your hurt. God forgives everyone who asks, so we need to be forgiving as well.

LET'S TALK

Ask your kids!

When was the last time you forgave someone?

Does forgiving ever get easier?

Ask your parents!

FAMILY FUN
LOOK FOR IT

Jesus says we have to forgive others not once, not twice, but how many times? Use the clues below to find a Scripture reference and look up the answer.

- Not Mark, Luke, or John, but _____. (This is the book of the Bible you need to look in.)
- Nine plus nine equals _____. (Which chapter will you go to?)
- One half hour minus eight minutes equals how many minutes? (This is your verse.)

But you still forgive me, right?

You keep eating all my food!

WEEKLY CHALLENGE

Have fun playing a game of musical chairs and trying to sit in a chair before your family members do. When a person is left without a chair, the rest should say, "We're sorry." Then the person who is out should reply, "I forgive you."

Talk about why forgiveness is important. Is it always easy to forgive?

Maybe there is someone who has hurt you. What can you do to forgive that person this week?

Jesus had much to say about forgiveness and other things. Read His Sermon on the Mount in Matthew 5–7.

✔

CHECKPOINT!

We learned that God wants us to forgive, even when we don't feel like it.

153

MEMORY VERSE

"I am the vine; you are the branches. The one who remains in Me and I in him produces much fruit, because you can do nothing without Me."

–John 15:5

BROKEN BRANCHES

The McDougal family loves cherries. Cherry pie, cherry cake, cherry jam, cherry pancakes–cherry anything. If it tastes good with cherries, Mrs. McDougal makes it.

The fun part of liking cherries is picking them. Every summer the McDougals take a lovely drive through the countryside to Mr. Thompson's Cherry Orchard. When they arrive, they get big, white buckets. Then they go into the orchard and pick ripe cherries off the trees.

Last year when the McDougals arrived at the orchard, they saw a big sign. It said CLOSED. Mr. Thompson just happened to be outside.

"Why are you closed?" Mr. McDougal called to him.

"Storm," Mr. Thompson said walking toward the McDougals' car. "A big storm came through. Ripped the branches off the trees. The fruit is dead, and the orchard is ruined."

Good fruit only grows when the branches are connected to the trees. The trees give the branches life. Once the branches are torn from the trees, the fruit on them dies.

Have you ever thought that Jesus is like a big, strong tree, and we are like His branches? Sin would love to come along, like a storm, and tear us away from Jesus. But God gives us the power to say no to sin. If we say no, God promises that we will always be connected to Jesus, and being connected to Jesus produces good fruit. Not the kind of fruit we eat, but good things like love, joy, peace, patience, kindness, goodness, faith, gentleness, and self-control. We get those blessings by staying connected to Jesus and growing strong in Him.

Hopefully Mr. Thompson will see the branches of his cherry trees filled with fruit once again. The McDougals definitely hope so! Those orchard trees are a great reminder that fruit is a blessing–the kind that grows on branches and especially the kind that grows in our hearts.

Ask your kids!

LET'S TALK

What happens if we allow ourselves to get separated from Jesus?

Do you think that I'm growing good fruit in my heart?

Ask your parents!

FAMILY FUN

CRAFTY CREATION

Draw a picture of a fruit tree. It can be any kind of fruit you want. You can even make up a new kind of fruit if you like. Add a piece of fruit on the tree for each member of your family. Write their names inside the fruit.

Plant a seed this week, either inside in a pot or outside in the garden. (Mom or Dad, check the Internet or another source for the easiest seeds to grow in your area.) Plant the seed carefully using good soil. Talk about the best ways to care for your seed. Then promise to take good care of it and help it grow into a big, strong plant.

Remember that God's words in the Bible are like seeds. How does staying close to God help those seeds grow? When you memorize Bible verses, it is like planting God's seeds in your heart. When the Word of God is in your heart, it helps you grow good behavior. You learn right from wrong and behave in ways that

are pleasing to God. When others see how strong you are in your faith and how well you behave, they will want God's Word in their hearts too.

Read Jesus' story about a man planting seeds in Matthew 13:1-23; Mark 4:1-20; and Luke 8.

✓ CHECKPOINT!

We learned that staying connected to Jesus helps us do what is right and good.

157

MEMORY VERSE

Every generous act
and every perfect gift
is from above, coming
down from the Father.

—James 1:17

AM I ENOUGH?

I'm not fast enough."

"I'm not strong enough."

"I'm not smart enough."

"I'm not good enough."

Have you heard those things playing in your head? It's not you talking to yourself. It's Satan trying to discourage you. Do you want to run a race? Satan says, "You're not fast enough." Do you want to stand up to a bully? Satan says, "You're not strong enough." Do you want to do better in school? Satan says, "You're not smart enough." The more you listen to what Satan says, the more you believe you're not good enough. And that's not true at all!

Jesus says, "I'm good enough, and I love you no matter what," and He will help you be your best. Jesus has a way of taking little things and growing them into something great. If you can't run fast enough, give your "not enough" to Him, and ask Him to help you run faster. If you don't feel strong enough against something in your way, give that not enough to Jesus too. Trust Him to give you strength. And give that "not smart enough" to Jesus. Trust Him to help you.

When God made you, He put inside you the will to stand up to whatever gets in your way. He blessed you with the ability to do many wonderful things, and He loves you even if you aren't the best at them all. Your job is to put all of your faith in Him and try your hardest to do your best. Don't try to be like someone else. Just be the very best you that you can be. Trust Him to help you.

This week's memory verse reminds us that God is generous with His gifts. He gives you whatever you need to be your best. God loves you so much, and He wants nothing but good things for you.

The next time Satan says that you're not good enough, then this is what you should do: Stand up to him and say, "Jesus is good enough, and that's all that matters. He died for my sins, and He loves me whether I'm the best or not."

Then believe it, because it's the truth.

Do you ever think you're not good enough?

Ask your kids!

Do you think I'm good enough to do big things?

Ask your parents!

FAMILY FUN
LOOK FOR IT

Confidence is the belief that you can do something well. What does the Bible say about having confidence? Let's look for it.

- Go to the last book in the Bible. Then start going backward until you find a book that begins with the letter *H*. (That's the book you need to look in.)
- How many years are in one decade? (That's your chapter.)
- Add up the years in three decades. Then add the number five. (That's your verse!)

Is a decade a long time?

WEEKLY CHALLENGE

YOU ARE GOOD ENOUGH !

This week, your challenge is to boost someone's confidence. You can do that by sharing God's gifts of patience, kindness, gentleness, and love. Watch how God takes these simple gifts and turns them into something great.

Look for opportunities to say, "Good job!" or "You're trying really hard" or "Wow, you are really getting better." Be gentle, kind, patient, and loving with your confidence boosting. Along with saying nice things, can you think of other ways to help your family and friends feel good about themselves? At the end of the week, talk about how it felt to help boost someone's confidence.

Do you always think you are good enough? What can you do to remember that you are?

See what happened when a little boy gave Jesus his "not enough" in Matthew 14:13–21; Mark 6:30–44; Luke 9:10–17; and John 6:1–14.

✔ CHECKPOINT!

We believe that God made us good enough, and we thank Him for His generous gifts. ■

MEMORY VERSE

In the same way He also took the cup after supper and said, "This cup is the new covenant established by My blood; it is shed for you."

–Luke 22:20

WHAT IS COMMUNION?

Heather wondered why grown-ups sometimes ate a piece of bread and drank a little grape juice in church. She knew that this was called Communion and it had something to do with Jesus. But Heather didn't understand exactly what bread and juice had to do with Him. She asked her mom.

"You know that Jesus was nailed to a cross and died," her mom said.

Heather didn't like thinking about it. "It was awful."

"Yes, it was," her mom answered. "But it was also the beginning of something great. Dying in that terrible way was Jesus' greatest gift to us. He traded His life for all the punishment people deserve."

This part was hardest for Heather to understand. "Why do people deserve to be punished?" she asked.

"Because God can't allow us to think that sin is okay," said her mom. "He knows that humans can't help themselves from sinning, so God found a way to clean them up so they could get into heaven someday—there's no place for sin in heaven. God sent Jesus to take away our sins. When Jesus died on the cross, He took the punishment for all our sins. Then God said that the only way for us to get to heaven is believing in our hearts that Jesus traded His life for our sins."

That still didn't explain the bread and the grape juice, but Heather's mom wasn't finished yet. She said, "Jesus said, 'I am the Bread of Life.' The bread reminds us of Jesus' body on the cross. The juice is a reminder of Jesus' blood when He died in that awful way."

Now Heather knows, and you do, too, that Communion is one important way we remember Jesus' gift and God's promise that we will live forever in heaven. Communion is about our friendship with Jesus. Can you imagine a friend loving you enough to die for you? That's the kind of friend Jesus is, and Communion is how we remember and say, "Thank You."

What does Jesus mean to you?

Ask your kids!

What does Jesus mean to you?

When did you take Communion for the first time?

Ask your parents!

FAMILY FUN

BIRDBRAIN IDEA

Sit in a circle. The first person says, "I love Jesus because" and adds one reason why he loves Jesus. The second person says, "I love Jesus because" and repeats what the first person said and then adds her reason to it. Keep going adding on reasons to love Jesus until one player can't remember them all.

WEEKLY CHALLENGE

THANK YOU, JESUS

The Bible's New Testament is about something called God's New Covenant. Covenant means agreement. God asks us to believe that when Jesus died on the cross He took the punishment for all our sin. Jesus died so that we can be forgiven for our sins. And God promises that if we agree, then He will forgive us our sins and allow us into heaven.

This week, find a new way each day to say, "Thank You, Jesus!" It might be a prayer, a song, or a letter you write to Him. Remember Jesus' amazing gift and just how much He loves you.

Communion began with Jesus and His disciples. Read about it in Matthew 26:20-30; Mark 14:17-26; Luke 22:14-23; and John 13:21-30.

✔ **CHECKPOINT!**

We understand what Communion is and that Jesus died for our sins.

MEMORY VERSE

"Go, therefore, and make disciples of all nations, baptizing them in the name of the Father and of the Son and of the Holy Spirit."

–Matthew 28:19

FISHING FOR PEOPLE

While Jesus was on earth, He taught people about God and the importance of following Him. Jesus didn't do it alone; He chose twelve men to help Him. These were His disciples. That just means that these men followed Jesus, helped Him, and learned from Him. They wanted to live like Jesus—in a way that was pleasing to God.

Some of the men were fishermen. When Jesus saw them fishing, He said, "Follow Me, and I will make you fish for people!" (Matthew 4:19). What did Jesus mean by "fish for people"? That would take a really big net! Jesus sometimes spoke in unusual ways that made people really think. So think about it. If you want to attract fish, you use bait. What sort of bait could you use to attract people to God? God's love! Jesus wanted His disciples to learn from Him how much God loves us so they could use it to "fish" for more people—to bring more people to Him.

Jesus' disciples learned. They learned about God. They learned that Jesus came to save people from sin and that He is the only way to heaven. The disciples shared what they learned with others. And those people shared it with more people. And people kept on sharing what Jesus said. Today, people still share what Jesus taught His disciples so long ago.

Now, here is the best part. You can be a disciple too. This week's memory verse is Jesus speaking right to you. He says, "Go and make disciples of all nations." In other words, get out there and do some fishing! Jesus wants you to learn all that you can from the Bible too. It is His story. Then Jesus wants you to share His story and encourage others to believe that He came to save them as well.

Will you be a disciple for Jesus? You will! Then get out there and start fishing. Tell your friends about Jesus and invite them to be disciples too.

LET'S TALK

Can you think of some people you know who teach about Jesus?

Ask your kids!

Can you name all of Jesus' twelve disciples?

Ask your parents!

FAMILY FUN

ACT IT OUT

Imagine that your best friend doesn't know about Jesus. You want your friend to know how awesome Jesus is and especially that He died for our sins and is our way to heaven someday. What can you say about Jesus that will make your friend want to follow Him? Act it out with a family member.

WEEKLY CHALLENGE

Here is a fun challenge for the entire family. Make a pretend television commercial to encourage people to follow Jesus. Use a smart phone or camera to record your video. You might even want to share it with others.

When you plan your commercial, decide what is the most important thing you want your audience to know. How can you get your idea across in a way that is both fun and respectful to God?

Read what Jesus says about making disciples in Matthew 28:18–20 and Mark 16:15–18.

CHECKPOINT!
We learned what it means to be a disciple.

MEMORY VERSE

So they said, "Believe on the Lord Jesus, and you will be saved—you and your household."

–Acts 16:31

AN ACT OF FAITH

Sam and his three friends went mountain climbing. The four young men had trained well and were strong and fit for the long, hard climb. With their gear packed, the men started off early in the morning just before daybreak.

At first they followed a rough trail up the mountain. Then they began climbing steep rocks. The men helped one another along the way. They climbed and climbed, higher and higher, until finally they reached the top. After they had rested awhile, they started back down.

The men used a rope to get down the steep cliffs. First one man. Then the second. Then the third. Sam was last. Just as he was getting onto the rope, his foot slipped, sending a shower of stones onto his friends.

"Ouch!" they heard him say. "I think I might have broken my ankle."

Sam was in pain and dangling above them on the rope.

"Don't worry, we've got you," said one of his friends.

"I'm not worried," Sam said. "I have faith in you guys." His friends worked together to gently lower him down to where they were. Then they helped him get down the mountainside. Sometimes Sam leaned on them. Sometimes they carried him. It was hard work. But Sam knew—he had faith—that his friends would do whatever it took to help him and get him back home.

Faith is such an important thing. When you put your faith in Jesus, you don't have to worry about what's going to happen in your future. You know that Jesus will do whatever it takes to help you and get you home to heaven with Him.

The memory verse this week is a great reminder to put your faith in Jesus. When you and your family trust Him, then your house becomes a home filled with faith. Whatever comes your way, you know that your own faith is made even stronger with family members there to help you, kind of like those friends helping their buddy Sam down the mountain.

Is your house filled with faith? It is if you all love Jesus and put your trust in Him.

LET'S TALK

Will it help strengthen your faith if your friends believe in Jesus?

Ask your kids!

Why is it so hard to have faith sometimes?

Ask your parents!

FAMILY FUN
LOOK FOR IT

Faith is a gift from God. Even a little faith is enough to do great things. How much is a little faith? Use the clues to find the Scripture and see what Jesus said.

- Something you wipe your feet on outside the door + a shade of a color = the name of the Bible book you should look for.
- S + the opposite of *odd* + t + *queen* − *qu* = the number of the chapter.
- T + *when* + a hot beverage = the number of the verse.

We have to think like they do, Charlie.

Wipe your feet? We don't wipe feet!

WEEKLY CHALLENGE

What is "mustard seed faith"? It is a little faith that grows bigger. Even a little faith is better than none. When you have a little faith, you begin to trust God. The more you trust Him, the bigger your faith grows.

This week, talk about how you can grow faith within your family—faith in each other and faith in Jesus. You can pray together. You can encourage one another. What are some other things you can do?

Finally, have someone take a picture of your family. Work together to make that picture part of a poster to hang in your house. Write on your poster: "We have faith in Jesus and each other."

Read about four more friends who had faith in Jesus in Matthew 9:1-8; Mark 2:1-12; and Luke 5:17-26.

CHECKPOINT!

We believe that faith is important and we help each other build up our faith.

MEMORY VERSE

"Be strong and courageous.
Do not be afraid or
discouraged, for
the LORD your God is
with you wherever you go."

—Joshua 1:9

NEVER FEAR—
JESUS IS HERE!

Tyler was probably the bravest kid in his second-grade class. Nothing frightened him, not fire drills or bullies, and not spiders or the occasional pesky wasp that found its way into the classroom. Tyler wasn't even afraid of tests. He didn't worry if his dad was late picking him up from school. When anything scary came along, Tyler put on his bravest face and said, "No big deal." Tyler was brave.

At least, that's what Tyler wanted his classmates to think.

On the outside, he looked brave and courageous. But on the inside, fire drills made Tyler's heart race with the fear that it was a real fire. A fourth-grade bully named Chad scared him. Big spiders and wasps gave Tyler the creeps. Tests were scary if he felt unprepared. And if Dad was late, Tyler *did* begin to worry. There was one more thing that really frightened Tyler: thunderstorms. The loud booms and flashes made him want to hide under his bed. Mom joked that maybe thunder was the sound of angels bowling in heaven and lightning was them celebrating when they got a strike. Tyler didn't believe it. At school, he sat bravely through a storm, not letting anyone know he felt afraid. But on the inside, Tyler was yelling, "Please make this go away!"

Wouldn't you like to tell Tyler that it's okay to feel afraid? Everyone is afraid sometimes. It's okay to let others know when you're frightened. Even Jesus' disciples got scared. When they were afraid, they called on Jesus, and He said, "Where is your faith?" Jesus asked that question to remind them that He is in control. Jesus is in control of fire drills, bullies, spiders, wasps, tests, dads, moms, kids, thunderstorms–everything! Jesus is more powerful than all of it, and everything obeys His commands.

The next time you are frightened and get that sick, shaky feeling inside, trust Jesus, and remember your memory verse: "Be strong and courageous. Do not be afraid or discouraged, for the LORD your God is with you wherever you go."

Do you think you are brave? Why or why not?

Ask your kids!

Other than you and Jesus, whom else should I trust?

Ask your parents!

FAMILY FUN

CRAFTY CREATION

Draw a picture of something that frightens you, but make it a funny picture. Are you afraid of bees? Draw a silly-looking friendly bee in a hat. Give a storm cloud a moustache. Or draw yourself looking afraid and then another picture of yourself with a happy smile. Remember: You can trust Jesus to give you strength so you won't be afraid anymore.

Fear is an emotion we don't like to talk about. We try to avoid thinking about things that frighten us. But talking about and learning to overcome fear is important.

This week, allow each family member to choose one fear that he or she needs help with. Then act it out. Show how other family members can help. Pick one person to play Jesus in the scene. Whoever is Jesus can show that He is in control and more powerful than fear.

Remember: You can trust Jesus and your family to help whenever you feel afraid. Say a prayer together, and give your fear to Jesus. Thank Him for loving you and being with you all the time.

Find out what Jesus did when His disciples were afraid of a storm. Read Matthew 8:23-27; Mark 4:35-41; and Luke 8:22-25.

✔ CHECKPOINT!
We know that Jesus is always with us, and He is bigger than whatever scares us.

MEMORY VERSE

Whatever you do, do it enthusiastically, as something done for the Lord and not for men.

—Colossians 3:23

TOUCHDOWN!

One Sunday after church, Julian and his dad were watching football on TV. The game was tied near the end of the fourth quarter. Their team had the ball, and Julian and his dad cheered as their players moved down the field toward the opponent's goalpost. First down. Second down. Third down. Fourth. The coach needed to make a decision. Go for the field goal or the touchdown. Coach decided on the touchdown. Julian and his dad watched enthusiastically as the center snapped the ball to the quarterback. They cheered when their favorite wide receiver caught the ball and sprinted over the goal line. Touchdown!

Julian noticed many of the players from his team jumping and celebrating in the end zone. But his favorite wide receiver was down on one knee with his head bowed.

"Is he hurt, Dad?" Julian asked.

"No, son," Dad answered. "He's praying and thanking God for giving him the ability to run fast, play well, and make that touchdown."

"So how come the other players aren't doing it?" said Julian.

His dad explained that not all players practiced what their favorite wide receiver did. He put into practice Colossians 3:23, our memory verse this week: "Whatever you do, do it enthusiastically, as something done for the Lord and not for men."

Dad said, "He gets it that God gave him the talent to play football, and when he plays, he does it for God instead of the cheers he gets from the fans. So when he makes a touchdown, the first thing he does is get down on his knees and thank God."

Julian thought that doing things for God and thanking Him for the ability to do it was a smart idea.

When God trusts you with the gift of doing something well, like He did that football player, He wants you to remember that the gift came from Him. In whatever you do, whether you do it well or not, you should always do your best for God. And always remember to thank Him.

LET'S TALK

What do you do well that you need to thank God for?

Do you know of any famous people who love Jesus?

Ask your kids!

Ask your parents!

FAMILY FUN

BIRDBRAIN IDEA

Jesus likes it when we decide to work hard and do our best.

You will need a ball for this activity. The idea is to pass it as fast as possible from player to player. Stand in a circle. The first player says, "I will do my best while _____ (and fills in the blank with something like 'studying for my spelling test')." That player tosses the ball to any other player, and that person promises to do his or her best at something else. How fast can you pass the ball? If someone drops it, you must start over.

WEEKLY CHALLENGE

The idea of doing a difficult or messy job might not leave you feeling enthusiastic—in other words, eager and excited. But this week's memory verse says, "*Whatever* you do, do it enthusiastically."

Your challenge this week is to work as a family to complete one big job that you have been putting off. Maybe you need to clean up the basement or a closet or tackle a project outside. You can do this! The challenge is not just to do it, but to do it enthusiastically as if doing it for God and not for yourselves. That means no complaining. Can you do it? When it's all finished, celebrate and give thanks to God.

A man told his servants to do their best taking care of his money while he was on a trip. Read what happens in Matthew 25:14–30 and Luke 19:11–27.

✔ CHECKPOINT!

We worked hard at something and did it for God.

☐

MEMORY VERSE

Put on the full armor of God so that you can stand against the tactics of the Devil.

—Ephesians 6:11

GOD'S SPECIAL ARMOR

When you love God and do all you can to please Him, the devil wants to get in your way. But if he does, you needn't worry. God has you covered! He gives you a special invisible armor that you can use to protect yourself from evil.

Have you seen pictures of ancient Roman soldiers? Roman soldiers wore armor to protect themselves in battle. The armor had parts: a helmet to protect their heads, a breastplate to protect the fronts of their bodies, a sword to fight with, and a shield to protect them from getting stuck by an enemy's spear. The soldiers also wore belts, and they had sandals on their feet.

Well, God's invisible armor has similar parts. Ephesians 6 tells us all about it!

The Bible says to put on the Helmet of Salvation (v. 17). That means believing that Jesus died for your sins and then rose from the dead. The Breastplate of Righteousness (v. 14) reminds you to always act in ways you know are right, like being fair, honest, and good. Your imaginary sword is the Sword of the Spirit (v. 17). That is God's Word, the Bible. You'll find the answer to any problem in there. The Shield of Faith (v. 16) gives you extra protection because faith in God protects you wherever you go. And don't forget your belt and sandals. The Belt of Truth (v. 14) reminds you to believe that everything in the Bible is true and helpful, and the sandals represent the Gospel of Peace (v. 15), reminding you to go bravely into the world and share Jesus with others.

Jesus wasn't afraid of the devil! He stood up for everything good, right, and true. He was brave wherever He went, and He was never shy about sharing God's Word. If Jesus saw someone doing wrong, He was courageous to step up and remind that person to do what is right.

When you remember to put on the invisible armor of God you will become more like Jesus and stand up to the devil, just like He did.

Will you do it? Will you put on your armor right now?

Why do you think the armor of God is important?

Ask your kids!

Have you ever seen a real suit of armor? What do you think it feels like to wear it?

Ask your parents!

FAMILY FUN

BIRDBRAIN IDEA

Faith
Peace
Righteousness
Salvation
Truth
Spirit

How well do you know the parts of God's armor? Using only your memory (No peeking at the story!) fill in the blanks with the correct words.

- The Helmet of _____
- The Breastplate of _____
- The Sword of the _____
- The Shield of _____
- The Belt of _____
- The Gospel of _____

(Your shoes!)

Have fun this week as each family member draws him or herself dressed up in a suit of armor. What will your helmet look like? Your shield and breastplate? There is no right way to do it, so use as many colors and designs as you want. You might even want to frame your pictures and hang them somewhere in your house to remind you to always wear the armor of God.

Did Jesus stand up to evil when He saw people disrespecting God's temple? Find out in Matthew 21:12-17; Mark 11:15-19; Luke 19:45-48; and John 2:13-16.

✔ CHECKPOINT!

We learned that putting on the armor of God helps us resist evil.

MEMORY VERSE

I no longer live, but Christ lives in me. The life I now live in the body, I live by faith in the Son of God, who loved me and gave Himself for me.

–Galatians 2:20

GIVE IT UP FOR JESUS

At his old school, Ricky behaved like a bully. He didn't like much of anything. He didn't even like his name, so he told kids to call him Rocky. He bullied anyone who didn't. Ricky got himself into plenty of trouble. He picked fights, talked back to his teachers, and got sent to the principal's office more times than he could count. Before long, Ricky became known as a bad kid in school, and he didn't like that! Ricky wished he could turn his life around. He even prayed and asked God for help. Then something amazing happened, a blessing in disguise.

Ricky's dad got a job in another city, and Ricky started in a brand-new school. The kids there didn't know that Ricky had been "Rocky the Troublemaker" in his old school. Ricky had a second chance, a fresh start. He acted in ways that would make God proud. He did his very best to be the best he could be, and before long he was known all over his school as "Ricky, the Really Nice New Kid."

Ricky isn't the only one who gets a second chance. We all do! God gives us Someone who can help turn our bad choices around for good: Jesus! When we give our sins to Him, He makes us brand new inside, fresh and innocent like a newborn baby. When we give our lives to Christ, we don't actually become a baby and live our lives again, but Christ gives us a new life by living in us, much like how Ricky got a new life.

Galatians 2:20 reminds us to live for Jesus instead of ourselves. Ricky gave in to sin, and he did what he wanted. Look where it got him—into lots of trouble. But you can learn from Ricky. Choose to obey God, follow Jesus, and make right choices. Give up what you want for what He wants. Then, just like Ricky, you will be the person God wants you to be.

Is there someone you know who acts like Ricky did when he was "Rocky the Troublemaker"?

Ask your kids!

Do you know anyone who turned his or her life around by trusting in Jesus?

Ask your parents!

FAMILY FUN
LOOK FOR IT

What two words did Jesus use to describe someone becoming new inside so they can get into heaven? Use these clues to find the Scripture with the answer:

- Go to the New Testament and find the first book that almost rhymes with *yawn*.
- How many French hens are in the song "The Twelve Days of Christmas"? (This is the chapter you are looking for.)
- Now go to the verse that is the same number of teaspoons in a tablespoon.

Mark?

Nope, that rhymes with *bark*.

WEEKLY CHALLENGE

Bring out the makeup, hairbrushes, face cream, and nail polish and have fun giving family members a make-over. Get a brand-new look.

It feels good to have a fresh look, doesn't it? It feels even better to be fresh inside and free from sin.

When we give our sins to Jesus, He comes into us and lives in our hearts. We will never be completely free of sin until our souls get to heaven, but when we live to please Jesus, we know that we are on the right path.

Talk about what it means to live for Jesus instead of yourself. Jesus gave it all up for us. He gave His life so we could live forever in heaven. What are you willing to give up for Him?

A man named Nicodemus once asked Jesus, "How can someone be born again?" Read what Jesus said in John 3:1-21.

CHECKPOINT!

We are grateful that God gives us a second chance to be free forever from sin.

MEMORY VERSE

If we confess our sins,
He is faithful and
righteous to forgive us
our sins and to cleanse
us from all
unrighteousness.

–1 John 1:9

WILL JESUS FORGIVE ME?

Kylie was quiet on the drive home from school. That was not at all like Kylie. "Do you feel okay, honey?" Mom asked.

"I'm fine," Kylie answered.

"Did something happen at school?"

"Mom. I'm fine. Don't ask me anymore."

At suppertime, Kylie's mom, dad, and brothers sat around the kitchen table talking about their day. Kylie said nothing. She played with her peas, swishing them around in her mashed potatoes.

"Kylie, you're so quiet," Mom said.

"I'm okay," Kylie answered.

"Are you sure you're not sick?" asked Dad.

"I'm fine! What are you all looking at?"

Her family was stunned when Kylie answered that way. Usually she was so bright, funny, and totally un-crabby.

Something had happened at school, something upsetting. Kylie had lied to her best friend. As soon as she did it, she was sorry. She apologized, and her friend forgave her. But Kylie worried; would Jesus forgive her too? Lying was a very bad thing.

Later that evening, Kylie confessed to her mom.

"Honey," Mom said, "of course Jesus will forgive you. He knows all about the lie. He was there. He saw and heard everything. Jesus knows that you're sorry and that you apologized. You can't hide anything from Him, but still He wants you to talk to Him about it when you pray. Ask Him to forgive you. You can trust Jesus to wash away that lie, and tomorrow you can start fresh and try harder."

So Kylie went to her room and prayed. She told Jesus about the lie. She asked Him to forgive her, and Jesus did. How do we know? Because 1 John 1:9 says so. It's in the Bible, your best friend, and the Bible never lies.

When you do something wrong, ask Jesus to forgive you, and He will.

Ask your kids!

When you do something wrong, what is the first thing you should do?

Did you ever want to hide a sin from Jesus?

Ask your parents!

FAMILY FUN

BIRDBRAIN IDEA

You need some bubble solution for this activity, the kind you get in a dollar store. Think about something you have done wrong, something you need to confess to Jesus (*confess* means to tell). Then close your eyes and say a silent prayer. Tell Jesus what you have done. Ask Him to forgive you and take away your sin. Then pretend that your sin is inside those bubbles, and send them up to Him.

WEEKLY CHALLENGE

Our sins hurt not only those we sin against but also ourselves and God. It hurts God when He sees us following our own selfish desires instead of what He wants for us. We need to apologize to Him for hurting His feelings. Asking God for forgiveness is another form of worship. It shows God that we depend on Him to help us, to take away our sin, and to make us clean again.

This week, talk about the importance of forgiving others and receiving forgiveness from God. Together, come up with a simple *I'm Sorry* prayer.

Remember: Church isn't the only place where you can ask God for forgiveness. He will hear your confession anytime, any place, anywhere.

Jesus met a woman in need of forgiveness. Find out what He said to her in John 4:1-26.

✔ CHECKPOINT!

We know that when we confess our sins to Jesus, He will surely forgive us.

GOD'S AMAZING GIFT

The McDougal family walked through a corn maze at a pumpkin farm. The maze was one of the best around. It had many dead ends. It was a tough maze to get through, but when you followed directions and found your way out, you got a reward.

At first, the McDougal twins, Emma and Liam, had fun running in the maze and coming to dead ends. But after a while, those dead ends weren't fun anymore.

"Are we lost, Dad?" Liam asked.

"No, not really," Dad said. "We need to do better at following directions."

"Maybe this will help." Emma handed her dad a brochure she had found lying on the ground. Right there on the back of it was a map showing the way through the maze and the only way out. In no time at all, the McDougals made their way through the maze and got their reward.

Our lives are a little like that maze. We reach a lot of dead ends along the way. And when that happens, we need help. We need Jesus. If we put our faith in Him, He leads us on the right paths away from those dead ends and toward something good.

People wonder why Jesus had to die on the cross. Think about it: What if dying was truly a dead end? Poof! You're gone. There's nothing else. That's what some people believe, but we know better! God sent Jesus to die on the cross to take our sin away so that we can live with Him forever. Jesus suffered the punishment we deserve. But that's not all. After Jesus died, He came back to life. That was to show us that we can live again, like Him. By believing that Jesus died for us, we can live forever with Him in heaven. It's God's gift to us, kind of like the reward the McDougals got for getting through the maze. Only God's reward is a whole lot better!

What would you do if you were stuck in a maze with no way out?

Ask your kids!

Do you believe for sure that Jesus came back to life?

Ask your parents!

FAMILY FUN

CRAFTY CREATION

You will need colored paper, scissors, and glue. Cut out eleven hearts all the same size. Then glue their edges together to make a cross shape. When you look at your cross, it will remind you that Jesus died because He loves you.

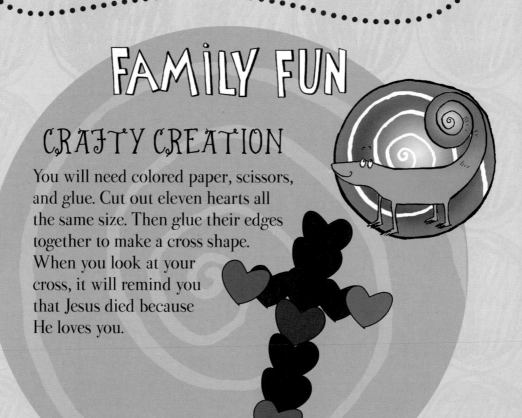

WEEKLY CHALLENGE

After Jesus died, His friends wrapped up His body in strips of cloth called a shroud and then put it in a tomb. They used a big rock to seal the tomb's door. Then something amazing happened. Three days later, that heavy stone had miraculously rolled away, and Jesus' body was gone! Imagine how His friends felt when they saw nothing in the empty tomb except strips of cloth.

This week, have fun wrapping up one, or all, of your family members from head to toe in toilet paper! Then break out of that paper shroud and shout, "He lives! Jesus is risen! He is risen indeed!"

Talk about why it is important that Jesus rose from the dead.

Read the story of Jesus' death and resurrection in Matthew 26:36–28:10.

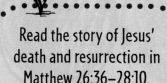

✓ CHECKPOINT!

We believe that Jesus died on the cross for our sins and came back to life again.

☐

197

MEMORY VERSE

He is not here!
For He has been
resurrected, just as
He said.

–Matthew 28:6

JESUS IN THE CLOUDS

Max loved learning about weather. When it snowed, he liked catching snow-flakes on his gloves and noticing that each was different. When it rained, Max had fun watching raindrops collect in the rain gauge he made in science class. Max enjoyed studying thunder and lightning, hail, sleet, and wind. But what fascinated him most were clouds.

Sometimes they were low and dark gray. Max knew that meant a storm. Sometimes they were thin and wispy like pulled cotton. Max knew that meant it was cold way up there. His favorite clouds were big, puffy, white ones. Max liked to lie on his back and watch them float by. Often they piled up together and formed shapes. That was the best part of cloud watching, the shapes they made.

One day Max and his mom were watching clouds, and she said, "Did you know that Jesus went up to heaven on a cloud?"

"He did?" said Max. "How do you know?"

"Because the Bible says so," Mom answered. "After Jesus rose from the dead, He stayed on earth for a little while. But then, when it was time for Jesus to go back to heaven and be with God, He went up to heaven on a cloud."

"That's so cool!" said Max.

Mom smiled. "And that's not all. The Bible says that someday Jesus is coming back, and when He does He will come in the clouds."

Max watched as another fluffy cloud drifted by. He imagined seeing Jesus riding it to heaven. "Mom," he said. "Where is Jesus now?"

"Jesus is alive, and He is everywhere," she said. "He is in heaven, but He also lives in our hearts, and His Spirit is here with us on earth. He is all around us, but we can't see Him."

"Not yet," Max added. "But someday we will."

Max is right. Someday we all will see Jesus. Most of us will see Him in heaven. But one day He will return to earth on a cloud. Then the whole world will see Him, and the people will shout, "Look, it's Jesus! He's come back again."

Ask your kids!

What is your favorite kind of weather? Do you like looking at clouds?

Do we know when Jesus is coming back?

Ask your parents!

FAMILY FUN

ACT IT OUT

We don't know when Jesus is coming back, but we know that He will. Imagine what that day will be like. People are going about their business, and then there's Jesus coming in the clouds! Act it out. Put on a little play about Jesus coming back. Will all the people be happy to see Him, or will some be ashamed for not living right?

You will find the story of Jesus riding a cloud to heaven in Acts 1:4–11.

After Jesus rose from the dead, He spent forty days on earth. He visited His disciples and continued to teach them. Before He went back to heaven, Jesus wanted His friends to know that He was indeed alive. He gave them instructions to continue to obey His teachings and also to prepare the world for when He comes back. Jesus wanted His disciples to tell the whole world about Him and to encourage people to live good lives. And His instructions were not just for the disciples; they were also for us. We can be Jesus' disciples and help the world get ready for the day He comes back.

How can you be a disciple? Everything you need to know is in the Bible. Learn it, and share it with others. It's that simple.

Talk about the reasons the Bible is so important. How can you use the Bible to get yourself and others prepared for the day when Jesus returns?

CHECKPOINT!
We know that Jesus will come back someday.

MEMORY VERSE

Then everyone who calls on the name of the Lord will be saved.

—Acts 2:21

HEAVEN HELP US!

Avery thought that Mrs. Davis was the best teacher ever. Mrs. Davis was patient and kind and had a special way of getting kids to learn. Avery loved her teacher, so when she heard that Mrs. Davis was leaving school for a while to have a baby, Avery felt sad. What would she do without her favorite teacher?

Her dad said, "Mrs. Davis will be back someday, but until then it's your job to continue to do well. Remember everything she taught you, and use it to help others. Learn from the new teacher as much as you can."

Dad's advice was wise advice, the kind of advice that Jesus gave His disciples.

When they heard that Jesus was going back to heaven, they felt sad and afraid. Their teacher was leaving them. What would they do? Jesus knew they were worried, so He promised them a helper called the Holy Spirit.

The Holy Spirit is God. You can't see Him, but you can think of Him in the same way that you think about love. You can't see love, but you feel it. That's what the Holy Spirit is like. It is God's love filling you up with His goodness.

The Spirit guides you through life and helps you do what is right. He helped the disciples after Jesus left. He gave them courage to stand up against those who didn't believe in Jesus and who hated hearing anyone talk about Him. With the Spirit's help, the disciples bravely preached about Jesus to anyone who would listen. They told them about God's love. This week's memory verse says that everyone who listened and believed in Jesus was saved from sin.

Do you believe in Jesus? If you said yes, then the Holy Spirit is with you right now. He is the One who helped the disciples. He helped Avery when Mrs. Davis left, and He will help you too.

Ask your kids!

How do people feel when someone they love goes away?

What does it mean to call on the name of the Lord?

Ask your parents!

FAMILY FUN
LOOK FOR IT

How do we get God's gift of the Holy Spirit? Use the clues to find a Scripture with the answer.

- A play often has three of these. (This is the book of the Bible you're looking for.)
- The number of thumbs you have. (This is the chapter.)
- 10 times 3 plus a word that rhymes with *gate*. (This is the verse.)

I need a little help with this one.

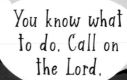

You know what to do. Call on the Lord.

The Holy Spirit speaks to you and will guide you. Listen to the voice in your heart and be sure to test what you hear by reading Scripture. If the voice doesn't agree with Scripture, then it is not the Holy Spirit. The Holy Spirit will always guide you to do what is right and what is in keeping with the Bible.

Talk about some of the things the Holy Spirit might say when sneaky sin tries to tempt you.

The Holy Spirit also helps you understand the Bible. Before you read it, pray and ask God for understanding. Practice doing it this week during your Bible study times. Talk about what you read, and see if the Holy Spirit helps you better understand it.

Spend time praising and worshipping God for His gift of the Holy Spirit. The Spirit will help you with that too. Try it for five minutes, praising God continuously. Feel His Spirit fill up your heart.

Read about what happened when the disciples received the Holy Spirit in Acts 2:1-46.

CHECKPOINT!

We praised God for giving us His Holy Spirit as our helper.

MEMORY VERSE

Therefore, if anyone is
in Christ, he is a new
creation; old things
have passed away,
and look, new things
have come.

–2 Corinthians 5:17

A CHANGE OF HEART

Sydney and her friends, April and Maddie, were eating lunch together. Maddie said, "I'm really worried. My little brother needs an operation." She told Sydney and April that her parents seemed very concerned. "I don't know what to do," said Maddie. "I just want to make all the bad stuff go away."

"You can't make it go away," said Sydney. "But Jesus can help you."

Sydney believed with all her heart that Jesus could do anything, and she wanted her friends to believe it too.

"That's not true," said April. "Jesus isn't real."

The girls disagreed about whether Jesus was real and if He could make bad stuff go away or help you through difficult times, and when lunchtime was over, Sydney felt very sad. After school, she told her mom about it. "April just doesn't believe," Sydney explained. "And that's never going to change."

"But I thought you believed Jesus can do anything."

Sydney was quiet. She did believe that Jesus could do anything, but she just wasn't sure that He could change April. Mom reminded Sydney of a Bible story, the one about Saul.

"Saul didn't believe in Jesus. He hated Christians so much that he had them thrown into prison. Saul's heart was full of hatred and sin. Then one day when Saul was walking on the road to Damascus, a bright light came from heaven and a voice said, 'Saul, why are you persecuting Me?'

" 'Who are You?' said Saul.

" 'I am the One you are persecuting,' said Jesus—"

Sydney knew the rest. Jesus changed Saul's heart and got rid of all its hatred, and then Saul believed.

"Mom," said Sydney. "If Jesus could change Saul's heart, I think He can change April's."

"That's right," Mom said. "Jesus can take hard hearts, broken hearts, all kinds of hearts and make them like brand new.' "

So, Sydney and her mom prayed for April. They prayed that someday April would love Jesus too, and they believed that He had the power to change her heart.

Do you think that Jesus changed April's heart so she believed in Him?

Ask your kids!

What do you think Jesus' voice sounded like when He spoke to Saul?

Ask your parents!

FAMILY FUN

BIRDBRAIN IDEA

You will need twenty blank index cards or pieces of paper. Print the word *OLD* on eighteen of the cards and the word *NEW* on the remaining two cards. Shuffle and place the cards facedown in four rows. Take turns turning over two cards at a time. If the two are anything other than both NEW cards, put them back facedown. The first player to match both NEW cards gets five points. Shuffle and repeat; play until one player reaches twenty-five points.

Second Corinthians 5:17 reminds us that when Jesus comes into our hearts, things change. We act differently and think differently when we live for Him. This week, think about things that need to be changed in your home, your community, and even the world. What can you do as a family to help make things better? Can you take food to someone who is sick? Or do some painting for an elderly neighbor? Decide to act on one of your ideas. How might you use the opportunity to share your faith in Jesus?

Read what happened to Saul on the road to Damascus in Acts 8:1–3; 9:1–31.

CHECKPOINT!

We believe that when Jesus enters our hearts, we become new inside, thinking and living for Him.

MEMORY VERSE

"Go into all the world and preach the gospel to the whole creation."

–Mark 16:15

ALL TOGETHER NOW

Leah hopped out of the school bus and ran toward her mom who was working in the garden. "Mom! Mom! Guess what?"

"What?" said Mom.

"Mr. Hopkins is starting a girls' hockey team. Can I play, Mom? Pleeeease? We'll show those boys who say that hockey is just for them. Can I, Mom?"

Leah's mom agreed to let Leah play. A girls' hockey team was a big deal in Leah's community. Until Mr. Hopkins made a plan for girls to play, hockey had been just for boys. Now it was open to everyone.

Some of the boys weren't happy to hear about the girls' team. But Mr. Hopkins said that they must be good sports about it. Those boys found it hard to allow girls into their sport and agree that it was for everyone. Still, they welcomed the girls because it was the right thing to do.

Jesus' disciples had a similar problem. Before Jesus went up to heaven, He told them, "Go into all the world and preach the gospel to the whole creation" (Mark 16:15). Preaching the gospel to everyone meant preaching it even to people they didn't like. Remember those boys who didn't really want girls playing hockey? Well, it was far more difficult for Jesus' disciples to invite their enemies to become Christians and to believe in Jesus too. But the disciples did it. They went everywhere and kindly invited even their enemies to believe in Jesus and be saved.

Jesus is for everyone! He welcomes boys, girls, moms, dads, aunts, uncles, grandparents–everyone, everywhere–to follow Him, and you can invite others to follow Him too. Just like the disciples did, you can go anywhere in the world and tell anyone about Jesus.

LET'S TALK

How do you feel about girls playing sports that are often just for boys?

Ask your kids!

What does it mean to be a Christian?

Ask your parents!

FAMILY FUN

CRAFTY CREATION

Work together as a family to make a poster that says JESUS IS FOR EVERYONE. Then frame your poster or laminate it and hang it somewhere in your house where guests can readily see it.

WEEKLY CHALLENGE

You are Jesus' modern-day disciples. His command to go into the world and share the gospel is for you too. Your disciple training begins with the Bible. When you read the gospels –Matthew, Mark, Luke, and John– you will learn to imitate Jesus' behavior and become more like Him. When you read the rest of the New Testament, you discover the challenges met by Jesus' disciples when they went out to preach to the world. Allow these disciples to be your teachers.

Your challenge this week is to make a promise to read your Bible every day, to learn as much as you can about Jesus, and then to share what you learn with others. The challenge for the rest of your life is to keep that promise!

The apostle Paul faced many challenges when he went into the world to preach the gospel. Read about him in Acts 13:1–15:35.

CHECKPOINT!

We promised to read our Bible daily, learn all we can about Jesus, and share what we learn.

MEMORY VERSE

Be alert, stand firm
in the faith, act like
a man, be strong.

–1 Corinthians 16:13

THE BIBLE IS YOUR BEST FRIEND

You have just taken an amazing trip with your best friend, the Bible. You traveled together from the creation of earth through days of ancient kings and prophets. You learned about God's plan to save you, and you read about the glorious day when Jesus came to earth. The Bible led you through Jesus' ministry and His crucifixion and resurrection, and it introduced you to great leaders of the church such as Paul. But just because you have reached the end of this journey, it doesn't mean the end of your friendship with the Bible. BFFs are best friends forever! The Bible is and always will be your best friend.

Think about your own friendships. Is communication important? If you and your best friend didn't hang out together, then you would lose touch and grow apart.

Satan would like nothing better than to separate you from the Bible. That's why 2 Thessalonians 2:15 says to "stand firm." It's so important to read your Bible daily. That's how you and the Bible remain best friends.

The Bible provides you with comfort when you are sick or sad, faith and hope when you are waiting for God to do something, and wisdom when you don't know what to do. The Bible is always there for you, and it will help with any problem or challenge you face. It encourages you and strengthens you. Best of all, the Bible tells you what God says–in His own words–and it tells you about Jesus, your Savior. Could any other best friend do all those things?

We have come to the end of this journey together, but it is only just the beginning of a brand-new one for you. If you continue to hang out with the Bible, the two of you will have a lifetime of adventures together. The Bible will be with you now, through your teen years, when you become an adult and have kids of your own, and even when you are old and gray.

The Bible is and always will be your very best friend.

LET'S TALK

What is the most important thing you have learned about the Bible?

Ask your kids!

Is the Bible your best friend? Why?

Ask your parents!

Best Friends Forever.

FAMILY FUN
LOOK FOR IT

God has an important message for you about His words in the Bible. Can you find the Scripture with the message?

- First, go to the Old Testament.
- Then find book number ____. (Rhymes with something honeybees live in.)
- To find the chapter, answer this question: How many days did it take for God to create the universe?
- June is month number ____ on the calendar. (This is your first verse.)
- Your second verse is the next verse.

WEEKLY CHALLENGE

Your final family challenge is for each person to write down the Scripture references for three favorite memory verses from this book. Then come together and exchange your Scripture references with a partner. Get out your Bibles. Who will be first to find all three verses and read them aloud?

I leave each of you with my hope that you will live the words and teachings of Jesus Christ every day of your lives.

May our Lord Jesus Christ Himself and God our Father, who has loved us and given us eternal encouragement and good hope by grace, encourage your hearts and strengthen you in every good work and word.–2 Thessalonians 2:16–17

Remember: Jesus is coming back! Read what Paul says in 2 Thessalonians 1–3.

✔

CHECKPOINT!

We know that the Bible is our best friend forever.

Remember:

Heaven and earth will pass away, but My words will never pass away.
–Matthew 24:35

Read:

Read Hebrews 13:8. You probably learned a lot about your family while reading this devotional, and if you try the same activities a few years from now, you'll learn brand-new things about each other. Why? Because we are all changing every day–even your mom and dad! But Jesus isn't. He is the same "yesterday, today, and forever." So all the wonderful things you have learned about Jesus in the Bible won't change either. Keep opening your Bible, and keep learning. Its wisdom isn't going away, and neither is Jesus.

Think:

1. Which memory verse in this book was your favorite? Why did you like that one the most?

2. Do you think you'll remember the verses you memorized? Think of three different situations where being able to quote a scripture would help you.

3. Ask each family member which weekly challenge was the most memorable. Are there any challenges you would like to tackle again?

4. New challenges can be fun! Make a list of five new ways you and your family can put God's Word into action.

5. The Bible is a friend you can keep by your side no matter where you go. What else makes it a good friend?

MEMORY VERSE INDEX

"LOOK FOR IT" ANSWERS

Page 12   Day 1–light. Day 2–water and sky. Day 3–land and plants. Day 4–sun, moon, and stars. Day 5–fish and birds. Day 6–animals and people.

Page 36   "Do not fear, for I am with you; do not be afraid, for I am your God. I will strengthen you; I will help you; I will hold on to you with My righteous right hand." –Isaiah 41:10

Page 56   The Bible describes God's Word as sharp like a <u>sword</u> (Hebrews 4:12).

Page 68   Your plans will be achieved (Proverbs 16:3).

Page 92   "Don't give what is holy to dogs or toss your pearls before pigs, or they will trample them with their feet, turn, and tear you to pieces."–Matthew 7:6

Page 104   Jesus is sometimes called the Prince of <u>Peace</u> (Isaiah 9:6).

Page 128   The story of (Jesus) is told in the (first) (4) (books) in the (New) Testament. Each one is named for a (man). What are their names? Matthew, Mark, Luke, and John.

Page 140   "This is My beloved Son. I take delight in Him. <u>Listen to Him!</u>"–Matthew 17:4–6